THE MUSIC OF WHAT HAPPENS

To
Richard Tobin, CSSR
amicus poetaque doctrina
atque optimarum artium studiis eruditus

John J. Ó Ríordáin, CSSR

The Music of What Happens
Celtic Spirituality
– A View from the inside

THE COLUMBA PRESS • SAINT MARY'S PRESS
DUBLIN WINONA, MINNESOTA

First published in 1996 by

THE COLUMBA PRESS
55A Spruce Avenue,
Stillorgan Industrial Park,
Blackrock, Co Dublin

SAINT MARY'S PRESS
CHRISTIAN BROTHERS PUBLICATIONS
702 Terrace Heights,
Winona, Minnesota 55987–1320

ISBN 1 85607 174 X

ISBN 0-88489-514-9

Cover by Bill Bolger
Cover photograph by courtesy of
The Office of Public Works, Dublin
Origination by The Columba Press
Printed in Ireland by Colour Books Ltd, Dublin

Acknowledgements

The author and publisher gratefully acknowledge the permission of the following to use material which is in their copyright: David Bolt associates for a quotation from *Helen Waddell: A Biography* by Dame F. Corrigan; T & T Clark for quotations from *An Introduction to Celtic Christianity* edited by James P. Mackey; *The Furrow* for two quotations; International Thomson Publishing Services Ltd for quotations from *A Celtic Miscellany* by Kenneth Hurlstone Jackson; Irish Texts Society for a quotation from James Carney in Vol 47, 1964; Peter Kavanagh for quotations from *The Complete Poems of Patrick Kavanagh*; Dr Bryan McMahon for a quotation from his translation of *Peig*; Mary M. Martin for a quotation from Helen Waddell's *Mediaeval Latin Lyrics*; Mercier Press for quotations from *The Field* by John B. Keane, *Early Irish Poetry* by James Carney, and *The Year in Ireland* by Kevin Danagher; Fr Peter O'Dwyer for a quotation from his *Céli Dé*; Oxford University Press for quotations from *The Irish Tradition* and *The Western Isle* by Robin Flower, *The Islandman* by Tomas O Crohan, and *An Old Woman's Reflections* by Peig Sayers; Royal Irish Academy for quotations from 'The Celtic Ethnography of Posidonius' by B. Tierney from *PRIA* vol 60; Colin Smythe Ltd for quotations from *Mediaeval Irish Lyrics* by James Carney and *The Voyage of St Brendan* by J. J. O'Meara; University of Wales Press for quotations from A. M. Alchin's *Dynamics of Tradition* and *Praise Above All: Discovering the Welsh Tradition*; Veritas Publications for several quotations from *Irish Spirituality* edited by Michael Maher; Wolfhound Press for a quotation from *The Wolfhound Book of Irish Poems*.

Contents

The Finest Music   7

Foreword   9

Chapter One   Celtic Spirituality in Twentieth-Century
                   Ireland: The Spirituality of Peig Sayers   11

Chapter Two   The Celts and the Celtic Fringe   22

Chapter Three   Integrating Christianity   36

Chapter Four   'An Exultant Spirituality'   51

Chapter Five   Word and Sacrament in Celtic Christianity   73

Chapter Six   A Radiant Creation   84

Chapter Seven   Both Sides of Death   93

Chapter Eight   The Way of Praise and Thanksgiving   106

Notes   111

Annotated Bibliography   117

The Finest Music

Once, as they rested on a chase, a debate arose among the Fianna-Finn as to what was the finest music in the world.

'Tell us that,' said Fionn, turning to Oisin.

'The cuckoo calling from the tree that is highest in the hedge,' cried his merry son.

'A good sound,' said Fionn. 'And Oscar,' he asked, 'what is to your mind the finest of music?'

'The top of music is the ring of a spear on a shield,' cried the stout lad.

'It is a good sound,' said Fionn.

And the other champions told their delight: the belling of a stag across water, the baying of a tuneful pack heard in the distance, the song of a lark, the laughter of a gleeful girl, or the whisper of a moved one.

'They are good sounds all,' said Fionn.

'Tell us, chief,' one ventured, 'what do you think?'

'The music of what happens,' said great Fionn, 'that is the finest music in the world.'

James Stephens, *Irish Fairy Stories*.

Foreword

In the late 1960s John Martin used to sing '*Cocaine*'. Substituting the word '*Celtic*' for '*cocaine*' in the lyric says something to me about the use of the term '*Celtic*' today:

I'll tell you a story about Celtic Lill.
She had a Celtic house on a Celtic hill.
She had a Celtic dog and a Celtic cat:
She even had a Celtic rat.

The modern Celtic craze offers us Celtic Oil, Celtic Insurance, Celtic Hampers, Celtic Chocolates, Celtic Festivals, Celtic Music, Celtic Churches, Celtic Spirituality and more besides. What special properties '*Celtic*' brings to oil, hampers, insurance and chocolates is quite beyond me. There is, however, much to be said for Celtic music, festivity and spirituality. As for the notion of a *Celtic Church*, in the sense of an autonomous Christian Church not in communion with the Roman See of Peter, it is a non-starter. It was far from the mind of such a towering Celtic figure as St Columbanus (d. 615), who wrote to Pope Boniface:

'For we – all of us Irish – who live at the edge of the world, are pupils of Saints Peter and Paul and of all the disciples who were inspired by the Holy Spirit to write the divinely directed scriptures, and we accept nothing beyond the teaching of the gospels and the apostles ... Our possession of the catholic faith is unshaken: we hold it just as it was first handed to us by you, the successors of the holy apostles.'[1]

The Music of What Happens elaborates on some characteristics and prayer formulae associated with that world to which the term '*Celtic*' is loosely applied, and focuses on the Irish experience of that world. While the content is serious, it is not without its light-heartedness – something in the spirit of the priest's house-keeper who provided the guests with 'an elegant and artistic arrangement of substantials and delicacies'. My hope is that the substantials will be nourishing and the delicacies enjoyable.

My sincere thanks to Fr Seán Ó Duinn, OSB, for much of the background material in mythological matters – chapter three – which were gleaned from his 1994 Kells Lecture, and a special thanks to Fr Richard Tobin, CSSR, for reading the manuscript and offering valuable assistance both as to content and presentation. I also offer my appreciation and thanks to the staff of the Royal Irish Academy, Dublin, the Louth Co Library, Dundalk, to all the authors quoted and to the legion who contributed to the oral tradition from which a great deal of the material is drawn.

May *The One* who is
    The guardian of the saints,   *(Sanctorum omnes,*
    The supreme ruler and Lord,   *Rector quoque Dominus,*
    The Bestower of eternal life   *Vitae Perennis*
    On those who believe in Him   *Largitor credentibus)*
continually surround us all with that delicate providential care which the Celtic tradition so beautifully hymns.

John J. Ó Ríordáin,CSSR,
Lá Fhéile Bhríde, 1996.

CHAPTER 1

Celtic Spirituality in Twentieth-Century Ireland: The Spirituality of Peig Sayers

For over fifty years and more the name of Peig Sayers is familiar to virtually every household of the Irish nation. Her years spanned the last quarter of the nineteenth century and more than half of the twentieth. Although most of her life was lived in the obscurity of a remote off-shore island, some very close friends who saw the depth of her culture and spirituality persuaded her to dictate a very considerable amount of material which they painstakingly committed to writing. As yet, only a small portion of this material has been published, but from that alone it is evident that Peig was a woman of greatness, exhibiting in her own unique way that vigorous spirituality which we now term *'Celtic.'*

Peig Sayers died in 1958 at the age of eighty five. The spirituality that fills her two published works[1] is typical of her generation rather than unique. It was the spirituality of the people among whom I myself grew up on the Cork-Kerry border in the south west of Ireland. And what was true for that part of the country in the early and middle twentieth century was true for much of rural Ireland at the time. While Peig's style and capacity for story is unique to herself, the underlying spirituality and cosmology emanate from sources common not only to her generation but to previous generations beyond number. What is immediately evident in that spirituality is a wonderful sense of unity and rhythmic harmony with the world around. The sky above and the earth beneath, the pounding of the ocean, the phases of the moon, the changing seasons, the bird on the bush, sunrise and sunset, are woven into a rich and sustaining tradition which speaks continuously of the glory of God. Besides, there is communicated a wonderful sense of time; almost a timelessness. All of this and more is embodied in Peig Sayers. Though illiterate, Peig was far from inarticulate, and her aesthetic sense and spiritual development are quite astonishing. Here is her description of an Easter morning in 1916:

> I was up very early because I had a good lot of work to do. When I put my head to the door, it would be a good person the delight of that hour wouldn't lift the mist from his heart. The sea was smooth and slippery, and the dew heavy on the grass and the sun beating over the back of Eagle Mountain as red as a piece of old gold. If I had pen and ink then wouldn't I describe well the delight of that morning. Many a nice colour I had to be seen with the rising of the sun – the gulls on the beach, the lark above me singing his pure gentle song and more, if I mention them.[2]

An introduction to a simple anecdote runs thus:

> It's glorious weather, Seán. The air at the bottom of the sky is as yellow as gold, and the reflection of the rocks is out in the water. There's not a breath blowing, but calm and beauty, and the fish so plentiful at the surface of the water. It is true for the poet when he made the rhyme long ago:
> > Praise and gratitude to you, Holy Father,
> > Who created the skies and heaven first
> > And after that created the big wet sea
> > And the heaps of fish in it swimming closely.[3]

And again:

> Many an old woman in Ireland had a nicer place and more pleasant to study than this, but I prefer this lonely place to any other place in Ireland. The golden mountains of Ireland are without mist before me. The sea is pouring itself against the rocks and running up in dark ravines and caves where the seals live. We are not disturbed by the uproar and noise of the city. There is a fine hedge around us and we are inside the Summer-house of Peace. There is no picture-house only these lovely things God created, praise for ever to Him! Every time I get a chance I give a run to get a view of these things which are most pleasant to my heart.[4]

Peig's parents were Tomás Sayers and Peig Brosnan. They were married in Ventry church and had thirteen children of whom Peig was the youngest. Peig, however, was in effect an only child, as there was no survivor beyond infancy from nine previous pregnancies. She was born in Vicarstown in the mainland parish of Dunquin. In the days of her childhood and youth she freely roamed the countryside which included her beloved Eagle Mountain. Having gone into service at the age of thirteen, she worked first in Dingle town and later for a farmer in the hinterland. In the first house she was treated kindly within the limits of the times; for a 'servant girl' was little more than a slave, and in all the three and a half years that she worked there, nobody offered the child an opportunity of making the ten mile trip home to see her ailing mother. In these confined circumstances, young Peig's only real friend and fall-back was the Lord himself. More than once he came to her rescue in direct answer to cries from the heart, and with the passage of the years, as happened with the young St Patrick before her, the bond between herself and her Lord grew deeper and stronger.

In view of the life she had in service, a suitable offer of marriage was more than welcome and wasn't turned down when it came. Before reaching the age of twenty, Peig married into the Great Blasket and, aside from her final years as an inmate of the County Home, she spent virtually all her days bounded by the sea. Looking across the strait to the mainland and at that mountain she loved so well, she exclaims:

> O Eagle Mountain, isn't it the stately, noble shape you have today on you! You are in the tied confusion of the years, but you show it not, for your form is as pleasing as ever. In the days of my childhood there was no other place under the bright sun was brighter than you. You were but a stone's throw from me then but the big watery sea is between you and me today ... O a delight to my heart was the smell of your heather! Often I'd pick a bunch of it and tie it into a fold of my dress. I'd never tire of sniffing the scented smell up in my nose. But now I've only the smell of the sea since I left you. It gives me peace of mind to be looking at your brow without mist.[5]

There is something reminiscent of the Bible's Gradual Psalms in all of this. Pilgrim Jews on their way up to Jerusalem would pray these psalms especially when they came in sight of the Holy City. They would see it on the hill and their thoughts would turn to the Lord. Peig's warm address to Mount Eagle soars higher yet, for she continues:

> O King of a Thousand Powers, 'tis many a thought you arouse in my heart. Am I not again a little girl, whilst I'm looking over at you, going from bush to bush looking for nests down along the riverside to the rapid of Coman's Head.[6]

And then, having been reminded of her own youth, Peig reflects on youth itself. Again, there is a sort of Biblical undertone to it; like something you'd read in the Book of Wisdom:

> What a gem youth is! Every nice thing is in her view. The difficulty of this world never daunts her. She doesn't like to be under control – she likes to be free, without tie, always. But isn't it quickly she goes! Do you see me today, children? I was once as airy as ye but as the skull said to the army officer:
>
> > As you are today I once was,
> > and as I am today you will one day be.
>
> Ye will too, if ye live for it.[7]

The lines attributed to the skull are in fact a direct quotation from the epitaph of Alcuin, that great clerical raconteur who was born in England, probably studied in Clonmacnoise, and lived out his life on the Continent around the ninth century.

Here is how Peig, the natural storyteller, introduced the topic of bringing home a load of turf from Iveragh:

> The weather is beautiful and the sun is shining brightly on sea and on land. There is freshness and brightness in everything God created. The sea is polished, and the boys are swimming down at the shore. The little fishes themselves are splashing on the top of the water and even the old people are sitting out here and there sunning themselves. Poor humans are overcome after the winter because we have a hard life of it on the island for that part of the year – hemmed in like a flock of sheep in a pen, buffeted by storm and gale, without shade or shelter but like a big ship in the middle of the great sea, cut off from the land without news coming to us or going from us. But God does the ordering, praise for ever to Him, when He sees our hardship. He abates

the storm, and gives us the opportunity to go among the people, and when the summer and fine weather like this come, He takes from us the memory and the gloom of winter.[8]

And here's the beginning of another story:

My love, my Lord God! Isn't it straight and smooth life goes on according to His true holy will! Shouldn't we be joyful for His glorious light to be lit among us! Isn't there still many a person lying in the dark! God with us, Lord, isn't that a pity! I understand that there is no more valuable jewel in life than to have love for God of Glory, for I have gone through life and I see a lot that reminds me of the great power of God. I am here alone in this lonely place, looking back on the pleasant life I have spent and thinking on all the people who were there in my time and who are gone on the Way of Truth. May God grant them the eternal rest! It's hard news if the bush is in the gap before us. But the sinner's benefit is to be for ever in love with God.[9]

So far, I have quoted at some length from the material that Peig dictated. Let me say a word about her now from other sources. The London journalist and writer, Robin Flower visited the Blasket Islands many times between 1910 and 1930. He learned Irish and has written beautifully about the islands and the people. Of Peig he says:

Big Peig is one of the finest speakers in the island; she has so clean and finished a style of speech that you can follow all the nicest articulations of the language on her lips without any effort; she is a natural orator, with so keen a sense of the turn of phrase and the lifting rhythm appropriate to Irish that her words could be written down as they leave her lips, and they would have the effect of literature with no savour of the artificiality of composition.[10]

W. R. Rogers, in his introduction to Séamus Ennis' translation of *Machtnamh Seana-Mhná*, says that 'students and scholars of the Irish language came from far and wide to visit her and she received them with natural country dignity. "I saw her being presented with a mushroom one day," a neighbour told me, "and she accepted it as if she had been presented with a gold cup."'[11]

It should be fairly obvious at this stage that Peig Sayers was a saint of God. She was not one to give the impression that holiness was beyond one's reach. Robin Flower tells how he was approaching the open door of her home one day and heard

> a clear, firm, woman's voice lifted in anger. I stepped over the threshold and was greeted in this fashion: '(May) the devil eat you between earth and sky! Get out!' I stood still in surprise, and was almost knocked over by an ass hastily decamping, with the owner of the voice following at his tail.
>
> 'God with us, is it you, Blaheen,' said she.
>
> 'It is,' said I, 'but what have I done that you give me to the devil to eat between earth and sky?'
>
> 'Ah! you know well it wasn't you I was cursing, but the ass, for he's the thief of the world, and my heart's broken driving him out of the house.'

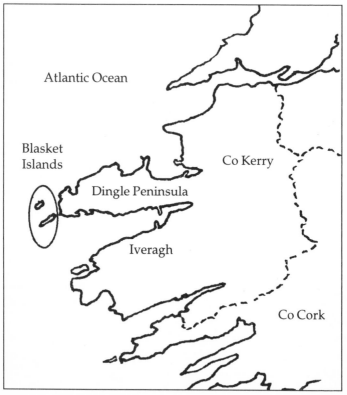

Location of the Blaskets in south-west Ireland

'The people of the island have a fine gift of cursing,' said I.

'We have', she answered, 'but there is no sin in it. If the curse came from the heart, it would be a sin. But it is from the lips they come, and we use them only to give force to our speech, and they are a great relief for the heart.' 'Well,' I said, 'I make little of them, for if the blessings come from the heart I don't care where the curses come from.'[12]

The island on which Peig lived – the Great Blasket – is really a mountain ridge breaking the surface of the Atlantic. It measures about three miles by one. The name is derived from old Norse and means 'a sharp reef or rock'; 'a crag in the midst of the great sea'[13] as Ó Crohan puts it. Scattered round about the Great Blasket are several small islands and rocks. The landscape reveals part of the story of the island with its prehistoric fort, early Christian cells, ancient church, martello tower, lighthouse, and the ruins of the little village on the cliff above the strand at the lea side of the island and facing the mainland. In the early twentieth century, the Congested Districts Board began a relief road on the Great Blasket but it was never completed because funds ran out. Many of the islanders were thought to have an ancestry on the island no further back than the mid-nineteenth century.

Peig is not the only chronicler of Blasket life. It is described also by Robin Flower, Tomás Ó Crohan, Muiris Ó Súilleabháin and others. The life so described would have been readily recognised by Neolithic or New Stone Age people of long ago. There were no shops, no craftsmen, no tea, sugar, flour; not to mention modern luxuries and inventions. Survival involved continual struggle, and nobody knew if the men who went down to the sea in curraghs at the dawning of the day would ever return. Starvation frequently stared them in the face, but the attempt to stave it off could, and all too often did, involve violent death on land or sea. Both Tomás Ó Crohan and Peig lost children violently. Ó Crohan at the age of 22 married Maura Keane in the church in Ballyferriter. They had a large family and Tomás buried every one of them together with his poor wife. Here is how he describes it in *An tOileánach*:

Ten children were born to us but they had no good fortune, God help us! The very first of them that we christened was only seven or eight years old when he fell over the cliff and was killed. From that time on they went as quickly as they came. Two died of measles, and every epidemic that came carried off one or other of them. Dónal was drowned trying to save a lady off the White Strand. I had another fine lad helping me. Before long I lost him, too. All these things were a sore trouble to the poor mother, and she, too, was taken from me. May God spare us the light of our eyes! She left a little babe, only I had a little girl grown up to take care of her; but she, too, was only just grown up when she heard the call like the rest. The girl who had brought her up married in Dunmore. She died, too, leaving seven children. May God's blessing be with them – those of them that are in the grave – and with the poor woman whose heart broke for them.[14]

Ó Crohan was no complainer, but a man of sturdy character and independence of thought. Peig, too, deserved the appellation *'Big Peig'* for she was a woman who was larger than life and possessed of a profound faith and richness of character. Straightforward but kindly in her speech, Peig had no illusions about any kind of idyllic life on an island. 'Since the time I was married,' she says, 'I have never known a day that I was entirely happy. My husband was a sick man most of his days, and then he died and left me, and I brought up my children … and I shall be alone in the end of my life. But it is God's will and the way of the world, and we must not complain.'[15]

Her great composure even in the face of danger and tragedy was surely a gift of the Holy Spirit. When the British army raided the island during the War of Independence, there was pandemonium and virtually everybody was in a state of panic. Peig's daughter rushed in with great terror on her and said:

'Oh! God with us, Mammy, all the soldiers and guns that are about the hamlet – and what are you doing?'

'I am eating, my girl,' said I. 'If it's death itself for me, it's a great thing to be strong for the long road.'

'I suppose,' said she, 'there will be no house or person on the island but will be burned to the ground.'

'Don't mind that, my pet,' said I. 'We'll all be together in the name of God.'

The word wasn't out of my mouth when Patrick, my husband, the blessing of God with his soul, came in, and mad rushing on him.

'For God's sake,' said he, 'have you no anxiety only eating and drinking, and your eating and drinking to be ended immediately. Hurry, and take down those pictures on the wall!'

(The pictures concerned were those of Thomas Ashe and the 1916 leaders.)

'Musha, defeat and wounding to those who felled them!' said I. 'They felled them without mercy and they alive, and it seems I have to hide the pictures of them now, and they dead! But may I be dead and as dead as a stone if I'll take them down in fear of any stranger wretch!'

'Take it down!' said he, angry.

'I couldn't,' I say. 'It will have to be left where it is, and if it's the cause of our death, it's welcome. They fought and fell for our sake, and as for Thomas Ashe's picture,' said I, 'I can't hide it from anyone.'[16]

This inner strength and the depth of her Christianity stood her well when her neighbours could not cope with the horrific death of her son Tomás. It was April 1920. The islanders had no turf due to the bad year. For fuel they depended on pulling and burning heather. At breakfast on the morning of Friday 20th, Peig and Tomás talked of Pádraig's impending departure for America. Assuming the role of a full adult, Tomás raised his right hand and assured his mother that he would see to it that she did not starve in the absence of the older boy. Without being aware of it, Tomás then did a *'turas bháis'* or 'death journey,' examining everything in the house in detail. Then after hesitating and meditating in the middle of the kitchen floor he went out, and that was the last Peig saw of him alive: 'When next I saw him he was calm and dead, laid out on a bier before me and the gentle bright hand he had stretched out so proudly to me in the morning was broken, bruised and lifeless.'[17] When pulling heather he fell over the cliff and having been dashed from rock to rock his body landed on a stone-slab hundreds of feet below. Peig herself was one of the last to hear of the accident, and having heard it, she could not move from the house because of her ailing husband who needed constant attention.

Recounting the sequence of events, Peig saw the hand of the Lord and his Blessed Mother at work in the ghastly situation, particularly in the circumstances in which the body was discovered after crashing down the cliff: 'There he was laid out as expertly and calmly as if twelve women had tended him. No one knows how he landed on that table of stone with the blue sea all around him. No one except God alone.'[18] The neighbours were too terrified to approach her and even those who brought home the body fled more quickly than they came, all except two. Peig set to work trying to give back to the body some presentable shape, and with motherly hands worked on the damaged scull until it looked human again. During all this time she 'prayed to the Sacred Heart and to the Holy Mother to come and assist me! … When I felt my heart tightening I took the statue of the Virgin and placed it on the floor beside me and from that moment forward I confess that I was but an instrument in the hands of the Virgin and her ohly Son.'[19] It was a real foot-of-the-cross experience and one of the most profound, harrowing and formative in her life. Referring to her time of grieving after Tomás, she said: 'I remember well when I was trying to work while at the same time the heart in my breast was broken by sorrow, that I'd turn my thoughts on Mary and on the Lord, and on the life of hardship *they* endured. I knew that it was my duty to imitate them and to bear my cross in patience.'[20] In subsequent years, she would tell the story many times over and her audience noted that she would invariably end with an invocation of the Virgin Mary and the words 'let everyone carry his cross.' 'I never heard anything so moving in my life,' said a Kerryman, 'as Peig Sayers reciting a lament of the Virgin Mary for her son, her face and voice getting more and more sorrowful. I came out of the house and I didn't know where I was.'[21]

Having spoken of the deaths of four of her children and the sorrow of their passing, Peig's profound faith is revealed in her vision of an ultimate destiny:

> But no one in this life is exempt from the law of God and it gives me pleasure to think that they are before me in the Kingdom of Heaven, and my prayer is that the God of Glory will grant myself and those of my children still alive never to break His law in this life in such a way as would separate us on Judgment Day, but that my little family will rise up from the dead about me and that we'll all be united in the Kingdom of God.[22]

Such spiritual riches stand in marked contrast to the material poverty all around. Towards the end of his book, *An tOileánach*, Ó Crohan said of his own circumstances:

> We have neither cow nor horse, sheep nor lamb, canoe nor boat. We have a handful of potatoes and a fire … Something or other comes to me now and again, one thing after another, that keeps me from starvation.[23]

Peig herself ended her days alone – as she had long since foretold – an inmate of the County Home in Dingle.

The last chapter of *Machtnamh Seana-Mhná* is the crowning insight into the depth and riches of Peig's spirituality. Out of her faith-filled heart and mind flows an uninterrupted and very beautiful meditative prayer. It is full of praise and thanksgiving, tinged with sorrow at the passing nature of this short life now drawing to a close, and yet ever so humbly confident in the God of Glory who has sustained her through hard times and good times with 'His royal sweetness'.

One may well inquire as to the source of this profound spirituality. Is it in the Celtic world of long, long ago? Yes, surely! but also perhaps in the millennium and a half of Bronze Age civilization which anti-dates the arrival of Celtic culture in Ireland as well as in the millennium and a half of Christian culture which has integrated with the Celtic way. Before exploring more deeply the spirituality that sustained Peig Sayers, then, we shall survey the evolution of the pagan Celtic world and examine how Christianity embraced, purified and transformed the pagan ways of this island on the fringe of the Celtic world. This is the subject of the next two chapters.

CHAPTER 2

The Celts and the Celtic Fringe

The generations typified by Peig Sayers were not self-conscious about their civilization although Ó Crohan did appreciate that he and his contemporaries on the Blasket Islands were at the end of an era. Living as they did with a sense of timelessess –

> He remembers names like Easter and Christmas
> By the colour his fields were[1]

– it was sufficient to speak of the past as 'long ago'; and that could mean anything from years to millennia. Both historical and mythological characters were as real to them as the neighbour next door and their affairs were discussed with keen interest. The people enjoyed a wonderful sense of place. Every field and mound and hill and rock had its own name and story. Of this I am sure as I, too, am of those people, and with each passing year and changing circumstance, I can identify more and more with the melancholy Scotsman who asked and answered his own question: 'Wha's like us? Damn few and they're a' deid!'

With the sense of place goes the sense of identity. When asking 'who are you?' in the Irish language, a person is not just inquiring after one's name. The question asked is *'Cér díobh thú?'* which means 'Of what people do you spring?' A person does not stand in isolation but belongs to a people, a community. Hence the surname is far more important that the first name. Today's world operates largely on first-name terms. This may give the impression of instant intimacy but it is superficial and indicative of the rootlessness that is characteristic of our times. There is no sense of identity, of belonging to a place or a family or a people. Only yesterday I heard of two wedding receptions being celebrated in the same hotel at the same time but in two different rooms. Both brides were first cousins living in the same city but totally oblivious of the fact that the wedding reception in the adjoining room was that of their nearest possible relative outside of the immediate family circle. Such a circumstance could not be envisaged by an older generation of Celtic people among whom the appreciation of family connexions were an essential part of understanding oneself. It is against this background, then, that we look more deeply into the Celtic world.

Of all the peoples who have settled in Ireland over the past ten thousand years or so, the Celts have left the greatest mark. Archaeologists variously categorise their predecessors as Beaker People, Food Vessel People, Urn People. Historians speak of their successors as Viking, Norman and English. But in the heart of them all stand the Celts. Despite the inevitable admixture of blood, Ireland is regarded at home and abroad as a Celtic nation. The term *Celtic* does not necessarily imply blood relationship. It has as much to do with culture as with kinship.

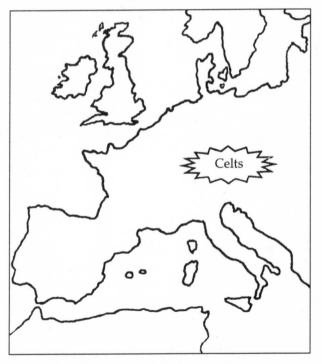

The Celts were strong in the heart of Europe
prior to expanding in all directions after about 1,000 BC.

On the wider European scene, the Celts emerge on the bridge between the prehistoric and historic periods. Racially they are categorised as part of that great mass of humanity known – for the want of more knowledge and information – as Indo-Europeans. Linguistically, the Celtic language is a version of Indo-European, and as such shares a common ancestry with virtually all European languages except Finnish, Estonian, Hungarian and Basque. Geographically, the first Celtic homeland corresponds roughly to the present provinces of Bavaria and Bohemia in the heart of continental Europe. And in terms of time, the Celts emerge in the late Bronze Age, that is to say, towards the end of the second millennium before the Christian era. By the year 1,000 BC they are found to be strong on the Rhine, and in the succeeding centuries they continue to expand in all directions – towards Ireland, Turkey, Spain and the Baltic.

The high point of Celtic domination in Europe coincides with the middle of the first millennium before Christ. This peak period is particularly associated with two very significant archaeological sites discovered in the mid nineteenth century. These sites – at Halstatt in Austria and La Tène in Switzerland – help greatly towards the creation of a framework for understanding how the Celtic world evolved.

In 1846, about 35 miles south east of Salzburg on the shores of lake Halstatt, the head of a mining group began excavating an ancient graveyard and uncovered as many as 980 bodies. Further excavations in the vicinity yielded a large number of iron artefacts and other articles of much interest to the archaeologist. The findings are assigned to the Early Iron Age – about 1,000 BC.

Around the same time, other exciting discoveries were being made at La Tène – 'the shallow place' – on the north-eastern shore of Lake Neuchâtel. Here, in 1858, a lowering of the water levels in the lake revealed not only the remains of wooden structures, but also large quantities of Iron Age materials including swords in decorated scabbards, spears and shield bosses, together with an astonishing variety of other objects including tools, coins, and ornaments. Like Halstatt, the site is Celtic and dates from the Early Iron Age but is later in time. Archaeologists broadly assign the various stages of La Tène culture from about 500 BC to the end of the first Christian century.

Despite their rapid expansion throughout most of continental Europe, despite their power and wealth, despite their early mastery of iron, the Celts never made a bid for empire. It would seem that urban and bureaucratic life held no attraction for them. The Celts were country people, living on the land and off the land, making the land their home, the basis for localised community life and the source of inspiration for their religious spirit. Although Celtic civilization glittered with exquisitely wrought ornaments, nevertheless it was characterized by an essential simplicity of life and was largely devoid of gross preoccupation with the accumulation of wealth and the possession of material things for their own sake. Their primary interest seems to have been human relations and living in the here and now.

Comments on the Celts by classical authors are often heavily dependent on accounts by Julius Caesar and Posidonius. More often than not, the comments come from hostile sources and must be interpreted accordingly. From these varied sources there emerges a picture of the Celts as being high-spirited, quick-witted, recklessly brave, prodigal, contentious, possessed of lyric genius and musical talent. Other characteristics attributed to them – notably by Diodorus Siculus, Roman historian of the first century BC – are: volatility of temperament, a tendency to exaggeration, vanity and bravado, a certain economy of words, and a marked preference for oblique rather than plain blunt speech – for hints, riddles and things half said.

Also in the first century BC, Strabo, a Greek geographer, writes that 'the whole race which is now called Gallic or Galatic, is madly fond of war, high-spirited and quick to battle, but otherwise straightforward and not of evil character. And so when they are stirred up they assemble in their bands for battle, quite openly and without forethought, so that they are easily handled by those who desire to outwit them; for at any time or place and on whatever pretext you stir them up, you will have them ready to face danger, even if they have nothing on their side but their own strength and courage.'[2] Speaking of the absence of fear in a person, Aristotle says: 'We have no word for the man who is excessively fearless; perhaps one may call such a man mad or bereft of feeling, who fears nothing, neither earthquakes nor waves, as they say of the Celts.'[3]

The classic commentators also inform us that the Celts wear breeches and cloak are great horsemen and fond of parties. 'When a large number dine together,' says Athenaeus, 'they sit around in a circle with the most influential man in the centre, like the leader of the chorus, whether he surpasses the others in warlike skill, or nobility of family, or wealth.'[4] Plato comments negatively on their drinking habits. As for the drink itself, we are told that the upper classes drink wine while the lower orders have to make do with a watery beer called 'corma'. The basic ingredients of corma are wheat and water with an occasional dash of honey. Athenaeus, the Greek grammarian who resided in Rome and a number of other Mediterranean locations, says that they 'use a common cup, drinking a little at a time, not more than a mouthful, but they do it rather frequently.'[5] Diodorus is less delicate in his remarks on the same topic and sees the Celts in Gaul falling easy prey to the greed of Italian merchants. He writes: 'They are exceedingly fond of wine and sate themselves with the unmixed wine imported by merchants … And therefore many Italian merchants, with their usual love of lucre, look on the Gallic love of wine as their treasure trove. They transport the wine by boat on the navigable rivers and by wagon through the plains and receive in return for it an incredibly large price; for one jar of wine they receive in return a slave, a servant in exchange for the drink.'[6]

The banquet seems to have been a most important social event among the Celts, both for the celebration of life and the unity of the community. Their appetite for meat was well noted as was their special *penchant* for pork, both fresh and salted. Hospitality was liberal. A stranger was not asked what his business was until he had eaten his fill. At the same time, personal honour was a matter of supreme importance and the deliberate or accidental slighting of or by a guest could suddenly erupt into a fight to the death. Such a life-style among continental Celts is corroborated by many ancient Irish texts.

Diodorus gives an interesting insight into Celtic battle-customs:

> For their journeys and in battle they use two-horse chariots, the chariot carrying both charioteer and chieftain. When they meet with cavalry in the battle they cast their javelins at the enemy

and then, descending from the chariot, join battle with their swords. Some of them so far despise death that they descend to do battle, unclothed except for a girdle ... When the armies are drawn up in battle-array they are wont to advance before the battle-line and to challenge the bravest of their opponents to single combat, at the same time brandishing before them their arms so as to terrify the foe. And when some one accepts their challenge to do battle, they loudly recite the deeds of valour of their ancestors and proclaim their own valorous quality, at the same time abusing and making little of their opponents and generally attempting to rob him beforehand of his fighting spirit.[7]

When the fight was over, however, the Celts were chivalrous in acclaiming the vanquished no less than the victor.

The ultimate victory of the disciplined and calculating Roman legions over the recklessly brave and flamboyant Celts was all too complete. Not only the culture but the language of the continental Celts has disappeared with the exception of a few fragments of Gaulish. Yet, in our everyday speech we use a variety of words deriving from Celtic roots: car, carpenter and lance, to name but three. The words 'rich', 'region', and the German 'Reich' all derive from the Celtic word 'rigion', meaning a kingdom. The word 'ambassador' comes from 'amt' meaning 'public office', while the Celtic word 'rix' meaning king, emerges in Latin as 'rex,' and in Irish as 'rí'. Finally, there is the word 'bardoi', whom Diodorus describes as 'lyric poets (who) sing to the accompaniment of instruments resembling lyres, sometimes a eulogy and sometimes a satire.'[8] (And from a combination of the Celtic words 'rí' and 'bárd' with the patronymic 'Ó' is derived my own surname, Ó Ríbhárdáin' – modern Irish, Ó Ríordáin; anglice O'Riordan – 'the king's bard'.)

During his conquering campaign in Gaul in the first century BC, Julius Caesar observed that his Celtic opponents were a very religious people. He then went on to note certain similarities between the Celtic gods and those of the Roman pantheon. Among both peoples there was no shortage of deities to be invoked and the names of over four hundred Celtic gods are extant. In the Celtic realm, however, the multiplicity of names does not necessarily mean a multiplicity of gods. In fact some scholars have argued in favour of a Celtic monotheism, but such a thesis is difficult to sustain.

Most honoured among the Celtic male gods is *Lugh* – 'the Shining One' – or to give him his full title, *Lugh Lámh-fhada*, 'Lugh of the Long Arm'. As with many other gods his sphere of influence is not clearly defined, but he is credited with being a master of many arts, a god of light and genius. His memory survives in such place-names as Louth in Ireland, London in England, Lyons in France, Leiden in the Netherlands, and Leignitz in Poland. The ancient Festival of Lúnasa bears his name as does the Irish word for the month of August (*Lúnasa*) which is ushered in by the festival itself.

The Celts deified the earth as 'mother'. The earth-goddess was *Anu*, source of fertility and abundance. Her name still sounds, often unrecognized, in the topography of her erstwhile dominions – Knockainey, Co Limerick, *Rinn Anna* (now Shannon), Co Clare, the town of Annan in Scotland and the river of that name, are but four of a host. Most striking of all, though, are the twin mountain peaks in County Kerry known as the 'Paps' – '*An Dá Chích Danann*' in Irish – 'The Paps of Anu.' In Celtic religious imagination these were the ample and beautifully proportioned breasts of the earth-mother-goddess.

Celtic veneration of the earth mother was often in triplet form under the titles '*matres*' or '*matrones*' – 'mothers', 'wives'. In Wales, for example, is the place-name '*Y Foel Famau*,' 'The Hill of the Mothers'. There are also the three mother goddesses of war, *Mórrígan*, *Macha*, and *Bodb*. These are known collectively as *Mórrígna* – 'the great queens'. The goddess *Brigit* is also presented in triplet form as are many others. In Celtic Christian Ireland female saints are often similarly remembered. In fact there are three saints venerated close to The Paps on the Kerry side of the county bounds and another trio – Latiaran, Trinity, and Iníon Buí – just a few miles to the east in Duhallow.

Gods and goddesses are likewise associated with wells, rivers, trees and sacred groves. The term '*nemeton*' meaning 'a sacred place,' is found all over the Celtic world. The druids of Galatia in Turkey met at 'Drunemeton', i.e. 'the oak sanctuary'. The word '*bile*' meaning 'a sacred tree' is also indicative of druidic rites. Springs, especially the fountainheads of great rivers, were particularly significant. There were Celtic sanctuaries, for example, at the source of both the Seine and the Marne dedicated to the *'Dea Sequana'* and *'Dea Matrona'* respectively. In Ireland, the Boyne, Shannon, Bride, and many other rivers are deified. Likewise in Britain the river Dee is deified as *'Deva'*, the Brent as *'Brigantia'*, and probably the Severn as *'Sabrina'*.

Bodb, who took raven form, was associated with death and destruction especially on the field of battle. *Donn Fírinne*, the god of truth, was the male god of the underworld. Even today, the catholic liturgy in the Irish language speaks of the dead as having gone *'ar shlí na fírinne'* – 'on the way of truth'. The Celts had no concept of hell. Under Donn Fírinne's rule the dead lived in a realm of joy and delight where one never grew old and the feasting never came to an end. Even the names for this 'other world' tell their own story: *'Tír na nÓg'* (the Land of the Young); the Delightful Plane, the Isle of the Blessed, *'An Tír fo Thoinn'* (the land under the waves). Caesar says that the Gaulish Celts believed in the immortality of the soul and in the transmigration of souls. And Lucan, the Roman poet, says of the druids: 'From you we learn that the spirit animates the body in another world. If your songs are true, death is only the centre of a long life.'[9]

Samhain, the feast at the beginning of winter, was chiefly associated with the dead, and the word itself may be derived from the Celtic *'sam'* meaning 'one' or 'together.' During the feast it was thought that the barriers between this world and the 'otherworld' were down, and that there was free movement for the dead to revisit their old haunts and homesteads. *Samhain*, too, was deified as a goddess of the dead. The influence of this feast has been far-reaching and deep in Celtic Christian spirituality – very probably giving rise to the Christian festivals of *All Saints* and *All Souls*.

As for the structure of Celtic society on the continent, we know that it had kings, but the monarchic system gave way in time to a three tier structure of nobility, commoners and labourers – the latter being either slaves or as near to slaves as makes little difference. Within the nobility, the highest ranking were the druids. Their role included that of priest, teacher, judge, diviner and counsellor. Druidic training took anything up to twenty years in the Gaul of Caesar's time, whereas in Ireland a twelve-year period was standard. Even where kings still ruled, as in early Irish society, they were in practice subject to the druids.

Besides the druids, there were two other groups in the top echelons of Celtic society. These were the *filí* and the *bards*. Because these were more concerned with the preservation of law, history, poetry and general lore than with anything specifically religious, they survived the advent of Christianity to Ireland. In fact Bardic Schools were a feature of Irish life down to the seventeenth century. Their art, too, was highly cherished as the Celts had an immense appreciation of eloquence. 'References to the eloquence of the Gauls and to their pre-eminence in oratory and polished speech could be multiplied indefinitely,' writes Nora Chadwick, 'because the Celts believed that eloquence was of greater power than physical strength, and also that eloquence attained its climax in old age.'[10]

The broad middle ground of Celtic society was occupied by the second grade or commoners. These were farmers for the most part. The bottom stratum consisted of a sort of slave class. Certain democratic elements and other balancing mechanisms existed in the Brehon Law so that the wheel of human fortune could turn; and it was possible for a family to go from slavery to kingship or kingship to slavery in about four generations.

Very little would be known about Celtic life were it not for the record of their impact on the islands of Ireland and Britain – particularly Ireland. The Celtic drift towards these islands probably began in the middle of the first millennium before Christ. Prior to this, Ireland had enjoyed about 1,500 years of Bronze Age culture. During this long and apparently peaceful spell, cattle and flocks were the basis of a sturdy economy. Trade-links existed between Ireland and all the known world. Bronze Age craftsmen skilfully plied their trade in gold, copper, and other materials, but their work manifests a certain lack of originality.

From about 300 BC we can discern the beginnings of a Celtic culture in Ireland, so that by the time of St Patrick's arrival in the fifth century AD it had almost a thousand years of tradition behind it. Archaeological evidence suggests that this Early Iron Age culture in Ireland was one of wealth and well-organized society. It had a socio-political structure of about one hundred and fifty petty kingdoms (*tuatha*) for an estimated total population of perhaps half a million. Some modern Irish baronies are more or less coterminous with the old *'tuatha'*. These kingdoms were structured so as to allow for a localised government with a wider unifying dimension. Thus, there was the king (*rí*) of the local territory (*tuath*); above him was a provincial king, and at the top of the pyramid was the High King (*Árd Rí*). The latter gave a certain unity to the political structure of life on the island but this did not always work out smoothly in practice.

The king, whether local, provincial or national, was not the law-giver. Laws were adopted by the people in assembly (*oenach*), only the freemen having franchise. This Celtic legal system (The Brehon Law) is the most ancient in Europe. It had fully matured in early Christian Ireland and operated effectively down to the seventeenth century because the Viking and Anglo-Norman invaders found it to be more equitable and comprehensive than any legal system of their own.

When the curtain of history went up, it revealed both islands, Ireland and Britain, under the sway of the Celts and speaking Celtic. In prehistoric times, Common Celtic became divided into what are called Q-Celtic and P-Celtic, the former associated for the most part with Ireland and the latter with Britain. The linguistic divergence came when one or other language group preserved or abandoned an initial *'p'* that can be written as *'qu'* or *'kw'*. For example, the Irish word *'ceann'* meaning 'head' is expressed in Welsh by *'pen'* – as in half a dozen headlands between St David's Head and Strumble Head, in south-western Wales. Irish (or *Goidelic*, the preferred term among scholars) was spoken by the Irish, and *Brythonic* by their neighbours. Brythonic seems to have been very closely related to Gaulish, which in turn would seem to be a cover-name for the group of dialects spoken over much of Celtic Europe. Cornish, Welsh and Cumbric all derive from Brythonic, while Manx and Scots Gaelic are rooted in Goidelic.

Due to the fact that Ireland was never occupied or conquered by the Romans, its early literature is a unique voice from that remote Celtic world which had in all other places been obliterated or subsumed into the expanding empire. The freedom from Roman domination was equally important in relation to the Irish language itself. Of that importance, Charles Thomas writes in his classic work, *Celtic Britain*, 'The Irish language, having gone through its

Primitive, Old and Middle stages, is therefore of enormous antiquity; both as a language and in respect of its early literature, its importance in European scholarship is much the same as that of Greek or Sanskrit.'[11]

The break up of Celtic Britain began with the invasion by the Romans in the first century BC. Then about the fifth century AD, Germanic tribes invading from the east began to change the map of Britain again and to isolate certain regions of it. Thus with the advance of the new invaders – Angles, Saxons, Jutes, Mercians, and others – Cumbria became isolated in the north-west and in its isolation the Brythonic language evolved into Cumbric. At the same time and for the same reason Cornish emerged in the isolated south-west. And because of the isolation of a large portion of the west, the Welsh language emerged from its Brythonic parent.

Welsh and Cornish were also influenced by invasions by the 'Scoti' or Irish. From the fifth century and possibly earlier, and continuing

The Teutonic invasions of the fifth-seventh centuries AD
isolated the peninsular areas of Celtic Britain

into the seventh century, considerable numbers of Irish established themselves in the western Welsh counties of Pembroke, Carmarthen and Cardigan. In North Wales, similar though weaker colonies established themselves in Anglesey, Caernarvonshire and Denbighshire. A plantation of Irish also took place in Devon and Cornwall; and it is probable that something similar happened on the Isle of Man, because this island was Brythonic-speaking up to the fifth century AD, but thereafter and down to modern times its language was Irish. The evidence for all this activity comes both from written and archaeological sources.

Within the same time-span (fifth-seventh centuries) another population movement which has a bearing on the map of the Celtic world of today took place. It seems that there was a substantial emigration of British Celts from the south-west of England – notably Devon. These people crossed the channel to Armorica which in time became known as Brittany and its language as Breton. Breton and Cornish were substantially the same until Norman times.

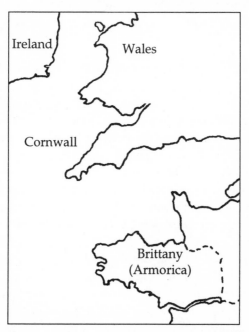

The name 'Brittany' in north-west France derives from migration of Celts from south-west Britain to the Continent from fifth-seventh centuries AD.

To complete the map of the Celtic fringe, we must look to North Britain where the most famous of Irish colonies took root and blossomed. This invasion probably began at the end of the fifth century when Fergus, Loarn, and Angus – three sons of a Co Antrim ruler named Erc – crossed over from their little costal kingdom of *Dal Riada* and occupied a territory more or less coterminous with the modern Scottish county of Argyll. It wasn't the first Irish colonising of the area but it was the most significant.

For centuries following, the Irish colony expanded and contracted with the tides of war until, in the middle of the ninth century, Kenneth MacAlpine finally absorbed the local peoples into one Gaelic kingdom consisting of all territory north of the Forth and Clyde. Its language and culture were Irish and it was known as *'Scotia'*, i.e. the land of the *Scoti* or Irish. The Irish (*Goidelic*) language and culture continued to spread in the tenth and eleventh centuries, even reaching the borders of England. This supremacy did not last very long and by the twelfth and thirteenth centuries both Irish language and culture were on retreat towards the highlands and islands where they survive, even if in reduced circumstances, to the present day.

From a general ascendancy over the first centuries of the Christian Era, the linguistic and cultural fortunes of Celtic Ireland and Britain declined throughout the High and Late Middle Ages. The Cumbric dialect probably lasted until the eleventh century. Cornish died in the eighteenth, but efforts to revive it are afoot today. Irish was spoken all over Ireland, the Isle of Man and most of Scotland until the late Middle Ages. Manx as an Irish dialect survived into the seventeenth century. In the same century, written Scots Gaelic began to diverge from written Irish, though separation had started in the oral form much earlier. Breton has held its ground well and so has Welsh, though since these are the weaker partners in bilingual countries, continuing decline seems almost inevitable. Irish remained dominant in Ireland until the late sixteenth century but has been losing ground to English ever since, despite the fact that it is constitutionally the first official language of the Republic of Ireland. In all, about two million people speak one or other of the Celtic languages today.

At a time of major change and uncertainty in the Irish Christian tradition, such as is evident today, what lessons can be learned from our Celtic forebears? Perhaps a clue to the answer is to be found in the theory that the elements which survive from the past are also symptomatic of what is most likely to survive into the future. When we rake out the ashes of a once glittering Celtic civilization, the surviving elements prove to be both rich and numerous as we shall discover in later chapters of this book. But from this present chapter we may note that the Celts were a strongly religious people with a profound appreciation of the aesthetic. They believed in life after death and the immortality of the soul. Local community bonding was deeply cherished by them while bureaucracy and centralised government were not. The Celts opted for simplicity of life with little inclination towards materialism. They were the rural people *par excellence*, in harmony with their natural environment. All of these elements and more besides were strongly influential in the evolution of a Celtic Christian spirituality and have survived the test of time. While being a key to the past, may they not also open doors to the future?

CHAPTER 3

Integrating Christianity

What I consider to be one of the great blessings of my life is to have grown up in a thoroughly Gaelic culture on the eastern edge of Sliabh Luachra in south-west Munster. My grandparents were speakers of both Irish and English; and while my parents did not have enough Irish to construct a sentence, there was a certain after-glow of the language in their use of the English tongue. My father in particular lived and died without ever knowing that words such as *'banbh'* (young pig), *'meitheal'* (work-force), *'Dia Linn'* (God bless us), *'flaithiúil'* (generous), *'tuile'* (flood, generous measure), *'go leor'* (enough), together with perhaps two hundred or more other words and phrases, were anything but English. Having travelled widely in Ireland and Gaelic Scotland I am of the opinion that despite the loss of the language in the earlier part of the twentieth century, the old Gaelic ways and culture were as strong then – or even stronger – in this Cork-Kerry borderland as they are in some of the Irish-speaking areas of today.

As with virtually all of my rural contemporaries, I lived quite unselfconsciously in a culture that retained characteristics and beliefs – albeit in residual forms – that would have made sense to our remote pagan ancestors. A prime example is belief in the fairies and the many folk-customs associated therewith. Even the Paps of Annan, visible from our front door, still figured regularly in our community life – though rather for forecasting the weather than for ancient fertility rites! Nevertheless, a certain numinous aura hung over them and the surviving customs and beliefs gave one a feel for a tradition that, though it had long been solidly Christian, was not without tangible roots in a pagan past.

To understand Christian Celtic spirituality to any degree, it is help-

Prior to personalising the forces of nature into gods and goddesses, it appears that the Celts believed in some kind of impersonal force lying behind everything there is – behind the objects of nature, the thoughts and actions of humans, the behaviour of animals; behind every movement of the birds of the air and fish in the sea. This impersonal abstract force or energy was perceived as filling the whole world and being beyond understanding. The word used to describe it is *'nert'* or *'nuirt'* in Old Irish, or *'neart'* in modern usage. It indicates 'force', 'power', 'strength', 'energy', 'dynamism', and the like.

Neart had a religious power and numinosity but was coldly indifferent and devoid of morality. It provoked awe but not prayer in any personal sense – no more than, say, the force of electricity today. Nevertheless it is this factor which underlies the Celtic Christian sense of the All-present God – perhaps the central and all-pervading concept in Celtic Christianity – God utterly near and immanent and at the same time utterly beyond and transcendent.

Personification – that natural need and creative intuition of humans – came with time. Personal divinities were found in land, rivers, and seas. The numinous presence in the land became a goddess, *Anu*. That in the sea became the god *Lir*. Personification extended to giving Lir a son, *Manannan Mac Lir*. In stormy weather, the white-crested waves are envisaged as the manes of Manannan's horses as he drives his chariot at furious speed over the surface of the water.

Many of these gods and goddesses are in triplet form or trinities. So, for example, the *'Lebor Gabála'* tells us that when the Milesian Celts landed in Kerry they were welcomed by the goddess *Banba* – the first of the three. She offered them possession of the country provided they named it after her; and so it was. The invaders moved up through Munster and met the second goddess, *Fódhla*, at *Sliabh Elbha* on the Limerick-Tipperary border. She bade them welcome and made them a similar offer on the same conditions. To this, too, they acceded. Finally, they reached the *Hill of Uisneach* in the very heart of Ireland where *Éire*, the third goddess, was awaiting them with the same offer and request; and since she gave them the greatest welcome of all, their druid Amergin declared that *Éire* would be the principal name of the country for all time. That is why Ireland, which has been known variously throughout the ages as

Éire, *Banba* and *Fódhla*, is best known as *Éire*, which is in fact the official name of the country in the Irish Constitution.

In the Celtic mythology the land of Ireland is envisaged as a fertile
woman. 'She is,' says Fr Seán Ó Duinn, 'the mother of the race who
feeds her children with corn from the fields, flesh and milk from the
cattle, fish from the rivers, and apples from the trees. She is the personification of nature.' Every time a new king was inaugurated, the
ceremony consisted of a ritual marriage of the king to the goddess.
This explains why there is no word in the Gaelic language for the
coronation of a king, and that despite the fact that there must have
been the inauguration of upwards of a hundred kings between, say,
the fifth and twelfth centuries AD. The ceremony was not a coronation; it was a wedding; and the Irish term for it was and is *'bainis rí'*
– the wedding of the king.

Since the wedding was a fertility rite in which the king symbolically
slept with and had sexual union with the goddess, it is hardly necessary to add that the inauguration ceremony had a lot of strong
and explicit sexual symbolism. At this point I must make a small
digression as I can never think of the *'bainis rí'* without recalling the
following incident. It happened in Galway during the 1984
Quincentennial celebration of the city's first charter. I was on a
preaching assignment in the cathedral where ten or fifteen thousand people were making the Solemn Novena to the Mother of
Perpetual Help. The cathedral and university being contiguous, I
also availed of the occasion to attend some archaeological lectures
being delivered to a class of mature students reading for a B.A. The
professor, Etienne Rynne, is always enthusiastic about his subject,
and is not beyond being a little outrageous on occasion if it is likely
to raise the hackles of his hearers or keep the interest-level high. The
topic in question and the mature nature of the class provided such
an occasion and the professor didn't mince his words in explaining
in some detail the symbolism involved in celebrating the king's
wedding at Tara. He hadn't long to wait for a response, because
Mrs Long – a sound and saintly middle-aged widow – interrupted
his flow of words with the admonition: 'Give over your nonsense
now professor! 'Tis above at the Novena saying your prayers you
should be.' With that, my friend Etienne, who had control of a powerful spotlight, swung it directly on to myself at the back of the audi-

torium, much to the amusement of everybody. What struck me so forcefully about the incident was the fact that it was a fine example of the combination of religion and daily life which is so natural to the Celtic peoples.

The tradition of the '*bainis rí*' is traceable back to the Land of Sumer in the lower Tigris-Euphrates valley where a brilliant civilization flourished about five thousand years ago. It spread across Asia Minor and into continental Europe and ultimately to Ireland. According to this long tradition, the goddess was not willing to accept any male. Her consort had to be young and vigorous, without physical blemish of any kind, just in judgment and rule, generous of heart, and an observer of certain '*geasa*' or spells which were not to be broken. If, for example, a king lost an arm or a leg in battle, he also lost his kingdom because he was no longer a suitable spouse for the goddess. Examples of this exist in the Irish tradition. Among them is the record of a stingy king who fell from the favour of his divine consort because visitors to the royal dwelling complained that there was no grease in their lives because he had given them no meat, and that they left his house with no smell of beer on their breaths! But once the king was to the liking of the goddess, she produced a rich harvest of grain and fruit and fish and milk and plenty for everybody. Thus were politics and religion combined powerfully in ancient Ireland.

The Tuatha De Danann gods and goddesses were associated not only with the fairy sites around the countryside but also with certain islands, among them *Hi Breasail* (The Isle of the Blessed), *Tír na nÓg* (The Land of the Young), *Mágh Mel*, (The Honey Plane – '*Mágh Mel* of the many flowers'), and *Máigh Dhá Cheo* (The plain of the two fogs/illusions). But whether on mainland or island, they lived an enviable life since they possessed three extraordinary qualities, namely, (a) the cloak of invisibility protecting them except when they wished to make themselves visible to humans; (b) a special drink which prevented them from ageing and dying; and (c) an unending supply of food from the '*muca Manannain*,' 'Manannan's pigs'. Pork was the favourite dish of the Celts, and Manannan's pigs were such that one could kill, cook, and serve them today and they'd be alive again tomorrow; so there was a never-ending supply of pork.

One of the major differences between the Celtic and Christian concept of the otherworld is the fact that the Celtic otherworld was accessible for temporary sojourns. One could visit it for a while and return to one's own home again. There are numerous accounts of otherworld travel by humans. Oisín, Cormac Mac Airt, Cú Chulainn, and many other heroes, visited the otherworld and returned. But some did not. A case in point is Connla Mac Cuinn who one day met a woman of extraordinary beauty (one of the goddesses), fell passionately in love with her, and having agreed to accompany her to *Mágh Mel*, boarded a boat of glass and was never heard of again.

In the matter of travel, the Celtic tradition in Ireland distinguishes broadly between tales of adventure (*echtraí*) and voyages (*iomrama*). It is to the latter category that journeys to the otherworld belong. This otherworld is envisaged as an idealized form of human life – beautiful food and drink, beautiful men and women, beautiful music, together with perpetual youth and perpetual summer. In the *Voyage of Bran*, for example, the hero is enticed by a lovely fairy lady who sings to him of that world far over the sea, with its thrice fifty beautiful islands – among them The Island of Joy and the Island of Women – a world where treachery and sorrow, sickness and death are unknown. The Celts had no concept of punishment after death. Donn Fírinne, the god of the dead, took his guests to an island off the coast of Kerry – *Teach Duinn* (Donn's House) – and there they stayed, feasting, we presume, in a life similar to that of the Tuatha De Danann.

The *Voyage of Maol Dúin* describes the visitation of thirty-three otherworld islands, one more fanciful than the next. It is suggested that the underlying objective of the tale may have to do with teaching people 'the "craft" of dying and to pilot the departing spirit on a sea of perils and of wonders.'[1] Certainly The *Song of Maelduin* conveys a mysterious, forbidding, and at the same time irresistible world:

> There are veils that lift, there are bars that fall,
> There are lights that beckon and winds that call –
> Goodbye,
> There are hurrying feet, and we dare not wait;
> For the hour is on us, the hour of Fate,
> The circling hour of the Flaming Gate –
> Goodbye, goodbye, goodbye!

Fair, fair they shine through the burning zone,
Those rainbow gleams of a world unknown –
Goodbye.
And oh, to follow, to seek, to dare,
When step by step in the evening air
Floats down to meet us the cloudy stair –
Goodbye, goodbye, goodbye!

The cloudy stair of the Brig o' Dread
Is the dizzy path that our feet must tread –
Goodbye!
O all ye children of night and day
That gather and wonder and stand and gaze,
And wheeling stars in your lonely ways –
Goodbye, goodbye, goodbye!

The music calls and the gates unclose,
Onward and upward the wild way goes –
Goodbye!
We die in the bliss of a great new birth,
O fading phantoms of pain and mirth,
O fading loves of the old green earth,
Goodbye, goodbye, goodbye![2]

When the Celts absorbed the Christian message, it was inevitable that there would be a certain carry-over from the old mind-set to the new. The *Navigatio Sancti Brendani Abbatis* (The Voyage of St Brendan the Abbot), which enthused late mediaeval Europe to rediscover America and to go in search of other lands, is a thoroughly Christian saga. However, within that tale the concept of hell, for example, as presented in the Judaeo-Christian tradition, undergoes major refinement due to the twin influences of the old pagan thought patterns and the new Christian liturgical cycle. It is related in the *Voyage* that somewhere in the arctic ocean Brendan encountered Judas Iscariot chained to a rock and lashed by the icy waves. Brendan did not at first recognize the lone tormented man so he ordered his crew to draw near and from a suitable vantage point questioned Judas as to his identity and the reason for his condemnation to such penance. 'I am unhappy Judas,' came the reply. 'I am not here in accordance with my deserts but because of the ineffable mercy of Jesus Christ. This place is not reckoned a punishment but as an indulgence of the Saviour in honour of the Lord's Resurrection.' The day in question was a Sunday. 'When I am sitting here,' continued Judas, 'I feel as if I were in a paradise of delights in contrast with my fear of the torments that lie before me this evening.' He then goes on to elaborate on his parole days out of hell: 'Here I have a place of refreshment every Sunday from evening to evening, at Christmas until the Epiphany, at Easter until Pentecost, and on the feasts of the Purification and Assumption of the Mother of God.'[3] The unhappy Judas adds that he is generally tortured in the depths of hell together with Herod the king, Pilate the Governor, and the High Priests Annas and Caiphas. Judas makes a final plea to Brendan that he intercede with the Lord Jesus to grant him an extra day's grace in honour of their meeting; and so it is granted.

Underlying the notion of a chance encounter between saint and sinner, together with a somewhat benign theology of hell, are two important concepts: (a) the pre-Christian understanding of a certain two-way traffic between this world and the otherworld which I have mentioned above; as well as (b) the notion that inhabitants of the otherworld, while not normally visible, were liable to present themselves in visible form at any place or time – a concept which will engage us in the paragraphs following.

In the Celtic understanding of reality, the gods and goddesses inhabited the hills, the mounds, the megalithic tombs, the forts, lakes, rivers, and woods. The entire world was enveloped in a sort of nature faith. People were always in contact with the otherworld, the world of the supernatural as it is called in other contexts. It was invisibly around one at all times and could suddenly manifest itself at any moment. There is an interesting episode in the *Tripartite Life of St Patrick* which throws light on his missionary approach to a people surrounded by so many gods and goddesses. Patrick meets the two daughters of Laoghaire at the well of Clibach near Rathcrochan, the royal seat of Connacht, and they begin to talk. The two princesses are washing their faces in the well when Patrick and his clerics come along in white robes. Never having seen their likes before, the princesses think that Patrick and his companions are of the Tuatha De Danann. Patrick begins to explain his new religion to

them and when the eldest girl, Eithne, finds her speech again she
has a lot of questions for the missionary. She asks them all in one
breath:

Who is God	(Cia bar ndíaeisi
and where is God,	ocus cia airm hítí?
of whom is God,	In inimh no hítalam?
and where his dwelling?	In futaemain no fortalmain?
Has he sons and daughters,	Inn amuirib nó hisrothaib?
gold and silver,	Inn asleibib no ingleannaib?
this God of yours?	In failet maic ocus ingena laiss?
Is He ever-living?	In fail ór ocus airget?
is He beautiful,	In fail immed cecha
was His son	maithessain (n)aflaith?
fostered by many?	Dic nobis eius,
Are His daughers	quomodo uidetur,
dear and beautiful	quomodo diligitur
to the men of the world?	(quomodo) inuenitur
Is He in heaven	si in iuventute,
or on earth?	si in senectute,
In the sea, in the rivers,	si uiuus semper,
in the mountains,	si pulcher,
in the valleys?	si filium eius nutrierunt multi,
Speak to us	si filie eius care et pulchrae sunt
tidings of Him:	hominibus mundi?)
How will He be seen,	
how is He loved,	
how is He found?	
Is it in youth	
or in old age	
He is found?[24]	

Now it is obvious that the princess is thinking in terms of her own
religion – the Tuatha De Danann faith or 'Creidimh Sí' – in which the
gods and goddesses were under the land, or in the land, in the
mountains, the lakes, the streams, the sea, the glen. Patrick does not
contradict her. Indeed he endorses, while refining and transcending,
her assumptions:

Our God is the God of all things,
the God of heaven and earth,
the God of the sea and the streams,
the God of the sun, moon and stars,
the God of the great high mountains and the deep glens,
the God above heaven, in heaven and under heaven.
And he has a household – heaven and earth,
and the sea and all that they contain.[5]

Patrick is here presenting the princess with a revised worldview. Rather than the impersonal concept of '*nuirt*' or its personalisation in a variety of gods and goddesses, he unfolds the mystery of 'The God of all things' revealed in the person of Christ. 'So,' concludes Fr Seán Ó Duinn, 'the ancient religion, far from being obliterated, has in fact blossomed into its fullness. Having gone through the impersonal stage of '*nuirt*' and the semi-personal deification of nature, it reaches its full development in the Incarnation. Nothing has been lost along the way.' God is still as near as ever. If one is to understand Celtic religion and Celtic spirituality and the folk-prayers arising from it, it is necessary to appreciate that continuity of thought.

A classical example of a prayer-form with its roots in the pagan past is the '*Lorica*' or 'Breastplate.' Several of these 'Breastplates' still extant are attributed to some of the best known saints such as Brendan, Brigid, Colman, Columcille, Gildas, Fursa, and of course, Patrick himself. Essentially they are 'protection prayers' in which the petitioner invokes all the power of God in the heavens above and the earth beneath as a safeguard against evil in its many forms, be it the activity of demons, magical powers, curses, spells, as well as more easily recognizable dangers such as being overcome by sexual lust, sickness, plague, famine, sudden death, poison, fire, drowning, malice of enemies, their sharp weapons, wounding, dangers on land and sea, wild beasts, thunder, lightning, hail, snow, rain, and whatever else there is in this world or in the underworld that can do harm to a person.

The '*Lorica*' of St Fursa, dating from the early seventh century, is still a popular prayer in Ireland:

The arms of God be around my shoulders,
the touch of the Holy Spirit upon my head,

the sign of Christ's cross upon my forehead,
the sound of the Holy Spirit in my ears,
the fragrance of the Holy Spirit in my nostrils,
the vision of heaven's company in my eyes,
the conversation of heaven's company on my lips,
the work of God's church in my hands,
the service of God and the neighbour in my feet,
a home for God in my heart,
and to God, the Father of all, my entire being. Amen.[6]

A shorter 'Breastplate' prays protection against the triple death –
wounding, burning and drowning:

God between me and the waters of my drowning,
God between me and the fires of my burning,
God between me and death without warning.[7]

The best known 'Lorica' is the 'Lúireach Phádraig' or 'Breastplate of
Patrick' and although it comes down to us in an eighth-century text,
it may well go back to the man himself. There is the possibility that
it may even have its roots in a pre-Christian incantation. Be that as it
may, according to Noel Dermot O'Donoghue, an acknowledged
expert on the Breastplate, it is 'one of the most remarkable single
expressions of Christian piety and practice.'[8] It is thoroughly
Trinitarian, combining the unity of God with the three persons in
God. It invokes the 'nuirt' or 'mighty power' but does so not simply
as an impersonal force but as the all-present and sustaining energy
of God. After the invocation of the Trinity, there is a plea to Christ
through the power of his Incarnation, his baptism in the Jordan, his
death on Calvary, his Resurrection on Easter Day, his Ascension
and the hope of his Second Coming in judgment at the end of time.

Then comes the powerful appeal to the densely inhabited world of
the angels and saints. These, who are normally invisible, are followed by the appeal to more tangible forces of sun, moon, fire,
lightning, wind, ocean, earth and rock. This is a Creation Hymn.
The world of the angels and saints is stronger and even more real
than the tangible earthly elements, for in the thought of the Breastplate, as Fr O'Donoghue points out, 'They are more real, for they
are eternal and indestructible, and their constant presence in
human life touches the immortal part of us. Their presence, creat-

urely and deathless, is a kind of token of eternal life. To invoke
these beings is to look beyond our mortal state.'[9]

The Breastplate also reflects a benign appreciation of the human
condition. Like John Eriugena in the ninth century, the author sees
humanity as fundamentally sound though not perfect. He does not
present us with a pessimistic Christian theology but views the
world as good, nature as good, humankind as good. Nor does a
Christian pray for help against the 'power' of the demon but
against 'the snares of the demon,' a very different concept, says Fr
O'Donoghue. The Christian has to be alert, as wise as a serpent,
nobody's fool, but assured that all heaven and earth will be respon-
sive to the one who asks. And here is a central insight into Celtic
theology: 'Christ comes not to show up or illuminate the deformity
of a fallen world, but rather to release a beautiful and holy world
from bondage; most of all, to release the human person, body and
soul, from bondage, and to dissipate the shadows that lie across all
creation through the presence of the enemy and his dark angels.
The new light of Christ is an enabling light, allowing the original
glory of creation to glow and radiate, not a new light to take the
place of that original light.'[10]

Despite the mystical enfolding in the 'Christ prayer' – Christ before
me, behind me, above me, below me, around me – the human person is not subsumed into the Divinity nor is the Divinity reducible
to a presence only in the person. The immanence and transcend-
ence, the nearness and utter otherness of God, are safeguarded; as is
the autonomous state of the individual, and all with the deft Celtic
capacity for keeping opposites in balance. It is the same Christ who
lives in me that lives in you:

> Christ in the heart of all who know me,
> Christ on the tongue of all who meet me,
> Christ in eye of all who see me,
> Christ in ear of all who hear me.[11]

'There is no privatism here,' writes Fr O'Donoghue, '– there never is
in the true mystic – but rather radiance and connectedness and a
deep holy respect for all human relationships. In this vision of
Christ in everybody, the whole of creation becomes luminous, and
the shadows of Satan are pierced if not dissipated … The man or

woman who has entered fully into the spirituality of the *'Lorica'* walks freely through a world where innocence and goodness are at home and where evil is an alien power from which there is nothing to fear.'[12]

Before concluding this chapter on the transition from paganism to Christianity, I wish to draw attention to one aspect of the transition which is surprisingly moving and shows a delicacy and compassion in the new Christian vision towards the old ways. A highly imaginative folk-story entitled *'The House of the Two Goblets'* addresses the pain and great sorrow involved in making the transition. During the Kells Festival of 1994, I listened with wrapped attention to Seán Ó Duinn, a Benedictine monk and fine scholar, as he unfolded the tale of a Celtic goddess of the Tuatha De Danann evolving to the status of a Christian saint. Eithne, the goddess in question, is torn between her friends in *Brú na Boinne* and the new religion. St Patrick is presented as being involved in a wordy tussle with the god *Oengus Óg* over the fate of Eithne. St Patrick wins, and as Oengus Óg and his retinue go away sadly without her, Oengus Óg recites a poem, the translation of which runs:

> Let us turn away in sadness from fair white beautiful Eithne,
> the bright gentle frail swan whom I used ever to protect.
> Let us depart, O host, to the land of promise;
> but though sad for us let us do it;
> sad to me the coming of this Patrick into this land,
> we will not deny it.[13]

After that, Oengus Óg gave a great cry of lament for Eithne. Every time she heard this cry she was very moved and upset. So she asked Patrick to baptise her. This was done and she received her own name at baptism. However, Eithne was very ill for two weeks and Patrick and his clerics were sad because of it. When Eithne perceived that death was near, she enjoined the protection of her soul on God and Patrick and said this poem:

> Call me, O people of heaven! I trust my soul to your entreaty;
> I shall not leave heaven now for the Brú of my foster-father
>   Oengus.
> I thank the Christ of the peoples for my parting from the Tuatha
>   De Danann;

Though I am of them, I am not of them,
I believe in Jesus the High King.[14]

And thus Eithne died and was buried by the Christian community at *Brú na Boinne*. 'There is a depth of pathos in the great cry of lamentation uttered by the Tuatha De Danann,' says Seán Ó Duinn. 'The author of the story shows an extraordinary sensitivity in the portrayal of pain and emotion; in the pain of the gods and goddesses as they see their way of life passing away. The pain of the Tuatha De Danann as shown in *'The House of the Two Goblets'* is the pain of humans as they see an ancient language or an ancient religion or culture disappear. Christianity can be presented as a triumphant march of the winners; but in the story of Eithne, we see the other side of the reality – the pain of the losers.'[15]

CHAPTER 4

'An Exultant Spirituality'

Two thousand years ago, Caesar said that the Celts were always looking for news. Two centuries ago, a German traveller in Ireland referred to the great attention the Irish pay to everything passing the streets. It is still the same. A spokesman on Radio Éireann – the Irish National Network – said in an interview that no matter how much news is broadcast, there are requests for more. I mentioned this fact during a parish mission in Aberdeen, Scotland, and was informed by a parishioner immediately afterwards that a regular greeting in the area is: 'Any little newsie?'

John Moriarty, the Moyvane philosopher, while not denying the Celtic *penchant* for news of any kind, maintains that the real hunger is for *'wonder'*: '"What great wonder?" – not "What's new?" – says Pegeen Mike in Synge's *Playboy of the Western World*. The poor people are hungry because they need wonder. We are all hungry for wonder. We're all Pegeen Mikes.' Enthralled by his hypnotic voice, one night in Galway I heard him expand further on this theme of wonder and the hunger for it that is in all of us:

> I'm thinking of an old woman in the long dark nights in the old days, in her dark clothes and her apron, and somewhere in the depths of her pocket are the rosary beads. And the rosary beads are about fifteen mysteries: five joyful, five sorrowful, five glorious; and every mystery is a new wonder; and she has the fifteen mysteries in the depths of her pocket; and she can pull them out and all the light of the world is there in her hand. She doesn't need electricity because she has fifteen mysteries; she has in her hands fifteen astonishments; and that's all the light she wants. And that's light enough for her in the dark nights after *Samhain*.

Such a woman was Peig Sayers. Her published work is shot

through with that mysticism of wonder of which John Moriarty speaks. Her life was far from idyllic in material terms and of this she made no secret; but she was rich in her capacity for contemplation and wonder: 'The people of the Island … are bitter poor, and they are in an island of the sea as in a prison, and must take the weather and the world as it comes to them, with nothing to make their lives soft and easy like those that are free in the great world.'[1] Yet this 'imprisonment' and grinding poverty didn't lessen her capacity to appreciate the wonders of nature and grace: 'Great as was my sorrow and heart-torment, God of Glory and his Blessed Mother helped me. I was often standing here studying the works of the Creator and tasting his royal sweetness in my heart. Everything he created was a consolation to me, even unto the grief itself, it would make me think deeper.'[2]

Many years ago, my confrere Fr Geoffrey O'Connell – God be good to him and all here mentioned – came in after a bout of Confessions on a country mission and remarked: 'I've been hearing mystics all morning.' His companion nodded to the effect that this too had been his experience. More recently, in the Hebridean Island of Eriskay, a man told me of a neighbour whom he had known in his childhood. She was living alone and well advanced in years. She lived wrapped up in converse with the Lord – chatting, and mumbling, arguing and gently chiding. Occasionally he'd pick up snatches of this divine converse: 'Why are you leaving me live so long? Look at the way Morag McKinnon died and she so young? I wonder why you let me linger.'

Some of these mystics can be more forthright. I'll never forget a woman in Limerick city whom I met in the course of house-to-house visiting on a mission. I was making small talk in the kitchen when I happened to glance up at a picture of the Sacred Heart. She spotted me and said in icy tones: 'I'm not talking to him!' 'Why not?' I inquired. 'Did ye have a row?' 'We did.' she replied. 'I asked him to do something and he didn't do it; so I decided to cool him off.' 'Ah,' said I, 'I suppose it was only a lovers' tiff.' Her face softened and through her smiling lips she said: 'Ah, sure that's all.' It was plain that the woman was on such intimate terms with Jesus that she could fight with him, or to use her own words 'cool him off'. There was no fear in her prayer, no disrespect. 'Love drives out fear.'

The freedom of relationship with Jesus equally applies to the Heavenly Father. God is the God of the universe and the God of the elements, but he is also the God who lives by the hearth and in the heart. A partial understanding of this intimacy may be derived from the Celtic notion of king (*rí*). When one's image of 'king' derives from a great monarch like Louis XIV of France or Henry VIII of England, there is immediately created an impression of being remote, not easily accessible, awe-inspiring; and as far as Henry is concerned at least, a strong element of fear may surface. Communication is likely to be indirect, self-effacing, through a third party. But in the Celtic world the concept of 'king' is quite different. In the small Irish '*tuath*' everybody knew the king. They knew his parentage, his relatives, his style. He was a native son, one of their own. This imagery strongly influences prayer patterns. The late nineteenth-century prayer formulae imported into Ireland were based on patterns of address to monarchs and potentates of the day. They were wordy and obsequious, and did not graft well into the Irish mind. It was this changed pattern of prayer, imported from Britain and the continent, that caused Fr Walter Conway, the parish priest of Glenamaddy, to complain: 'The prayers and the religious poems which our ancestors composed and used to repeat, have been given up ... pieces which came from the heart of him who composed them and went straight from the heart of him who said them to the ear of God.'[3]

This direct and familiar mode of address to the Heavenly Father does not emanate from any sense of having a '*right*' to address God so. Rather does it come from a warm trusting relationship such as Jesus had when he told us to say, 'Our Father who art in heaven ...' On the other hand, many non-Catholics wonder why we Catholics pray so much to the saints. No doubt there are learned theological reasons for it, but when asked, I simply reply that the saints are part of the family and that we're all on good talking terms. As for their images on the walls of our homes, it is but another way of displaying the family album. And how *wonder-full* it is to know that they share the home with us and are always *at* our side and *on* our side. Then too, I suggest that our habit of praying to the saints also stems from a certain gracious deference to the Heavenly Father. We may indeed have a '*right*' to speak directly to the Father but then there is also a sense of 'Lord I am not worthy,' or 'depart from me for I am a sinful man'. And for that reason we ask one or several of our sainted friends to act as spokesperson on our behalf and put in a good word with the Father. 'The Communion of Saints' is not just an *article* of the creed; it is a way of living.

While working in Drogheda I had occasion to take Holy Communion to an elderly woman who was house-bound, and, according to the parish priest, living alone. 'So you're living alone,' said I, on entering the house. 'Alone!' said she in astonishment, 'not at all!' And raising her hand to a variety of religious pictures hanging on the walls she continued, 'Haven't I himself? (the Sacred Heart), and herself (the Mother of Perpetual Help), and all of these? (her favourite saints). Alone? Never a dull moment.' The woman was neither alone nor lonely. She lived with the company of heaven in deep harmony, companionship, and contentment, immersed in 'the conversation of heaven's company,' as St Fursa puts it.

That companionship is as old as *Patrick's Breastplate* in Ireland and as old as the church itself. The Breastplate cries out:

> For my shield this day I call:
> strong power of the seraphim,
> with angels obeying,
> and archangels attending,
> in the glorious company
> of the holy and risen ones,
> in the prayers of the fathers,
> in visions prophetic
> and commands apostolic,
> in the annals of witness,
> in virginal innocence,
> in the deeds of steadfast men.[4]

The petitioner is summoning his heavenly friends. After all, why should they not come and help a person in need? For the Christian, even more than for the pre-Christian Celt, there is no impassable boundary between the material world and the spirit world. They overlap. It is simply that the one is visible and the other normally invisible. There is a unity of all things so that, as Noel Dermot O'Donoghue says: 'Not only was this world very close in a spiritual way, but it could shine through or otherwise impress itself on human perception. If one does not understand the nearness and apprehensibility of this 'other world' of the angels and saints, there is no hope at all of understanding Celtic Christianity either in its marvellous flowering in the 'Dark Ages' or in its pathetic and tenacious survival in what is left of that ancient faith and culture.'[5]

The affinity and warm love-relationship between the people of this world and the otherworld, as understood in the doctrine of 'The Communion of Saints', is well illustrated in a poem attributed to St Brigid. The work is that of an anonymous tenth-century poet who envisages himself as God's vassal, and rejoices in the thought of fulfilling his legal obligations in relation to lodgings and entertainment for his over-lord and entourage:

I would like to have the men of heaven
In my own house;
With vats of good cheer
Laid out for them.

I would like to have the three Marys,
Their fame is so great.
I would like people
From every corner of heaven.

I would like them to be cheerful
In their drinking,
I would like to have Jesus, too,
Here among them.

I would like a great lake of beer
For the King of Kings.
I would like to be watching heaven's family
Drinking it through all eternity.[6]

As well as being lovely in itself, this poem is illustrative of the Celtic Irish capacity to absorb ideas and images but rarely without adapting them to the native culture and environment. It is a refreshingly Irish presentation of the biblical heavenly banquet.

Love of nature and harmony with the environment are strong elements in the Celtic tradition emanating from this sense of the unity

and connectedness of all things. At times the Christian Celts have
been accused of pantheism – worshipping nature itself as a god.
This line of argument fails to appreciate the refinement of Celtic
thought and theology. For the Celts, God was certainly in all things
but not identified or interchangeable with all things. George
Congreve, preaching on Iona on the feast of St Columcille 1908, captured this element in the Irish tradition when he said:

> I think you will find in this saint (Columcille/Columba), and in
> the men formed by him, a remarkable confidence in nature, as a
> sphere which belongs to Christ by right, but waits for them to
> claim and hold for him in deed. They were not afraid of nature
> in her most dangerous moods, nor yet afraid of looking upon the
> seas and the rocks and the mountain pastures when the sun
> shone upon them, for fear they might love nature too much.
> Nature for them was not a questionable power, it was God's
> world, and they were God's children … Nature could never
> become for them God's rival, or claim the heart in place of God,
> for nature they recognized as the very kindness and love of God
> himself to men.[7]

Everything in nature was a reminder of the presence of God; everything was a gift of God; everything was a revelation of God. That, I
think, is why the Bull McCabe in John B. Keane's play 'The Field'
was so passionate about such a small patch of earth. It wasn't simply an expression of naked greed; that was there, but there was
more. He was grieving over what the new American owner was
going to do with that field – cover it with concrete – which the Bull
saw as downright sinfulness:

> I watched that field for forty years and my father before me
> watched it for forty more. I know every rib of grass and every
> thistle and every whitethorn bush that bounds it. There's sham-
> rock in the south-west corner. Shamrock imagine! The north
> part is bound by forty sloe bushes. Some fool planted them once,
> but they're a good hedge. This is a sweet little field, this is an
> independent little field that wants eatin'. A total stranger has
> come and he wants to bury (it) in concrete. It's ag'in God an'
> man …[8]

Speaking of the nature poetry of early Christian Ireland, Robin

Flower says that 'it was not only that these scribes and anchorites lived by the destiny of their dedication in an environment of wood and sea; it was because they brought into that environment an eye washed miraculously clear by a continual spiritual exercise that they, first in Europe, had that strange vision of natural things in an almost unnatural purity.'[9] This nature poetry consists for the most part of short poems and quatrains, often written on the margins of manuscripts. They attempt to put human language on nature's many voices of praise, be it of the elements, the bird on the tree-top, the animal in the undergrowth, the salmon in a shady pool. Each has a song to sing. Here are three of Flower's translations. They all refer to the blackbird (ousel) and the first is known as *The Blackbird of Belfast Lough* (Lough Lee):

> (i) The tiny bird
> Whose call I heard
> I marked his yellow bill;
> The ousel's glee
> Above Lough Lee
> Shakes golden branches still.[10]

> (ii) He whistles in the willow tree,
> Descanting from his yellow bill,
> Gold-beaked, black-coated, that is he,
> Stout ousel and his trembling trill.[11]

> (iii) Sweet ousel chanting blithely there,
> Where in the bushes hides thy nest?
> Thou hermit no bell calls to prayer!
> Thy soft sweet music speaks of rest.[12]

A poet of the early ninth century gives dates and seasons for the comings and goings and singing patterns of a variety of migratory birds – swallows, cuckoo, wild geese. These he ties in with the feast days of a number of saints. And then in the last stanza comes the whole purpose of all this activity in nature:

> Melodious music the birds perform
> to the King of the heaven of the clouds,
> Praising the radiant King
> Hark from afar the choir of the birds.[13]

Skipping from the ninth century to the twentieth, we find Patrick
Kavanagh entering into the spirit of early Spring in his *March*:

> The trees were in suspense,
> Listening with an intense
> Anxiety for the Word
> That in the Beginning stirred
> The dark-branched Tree
> Of Humanity …
>
> The blackbird of the yew
> Alone broke the two
> Minutes silence
> With a new poem's violence.
> A tomboy scare that drove
> Faint thoughts of active love.[14]

May is the month when Ireland becomes a garden, a glorious
national park. Of it Kavanagh writes:

> May came and every shabby phoenix flapped
> A coloured rag in lieu of shining wings;
> In school bad manners spat and went unslapped –
> schoolmistress Fancy dreamt of other things.
>
> The lilac blossomed for a day or two
> Gaily, and then grew weary of her fame.
> Plough-horses out on grass could now pursue
> The pleasures of the very mute and tame.
>
> A light that might be mystic or a fraud
> Played on far hills beyond all common sight,
> And some men said that it was Adam's God
> As Adam saw before the apple-bite …[15]

The blackbird and the lark vie with one another for the place of
honour in the Celtic Irish tradition. While I love both dearly, it is the
lark that transports me on its wings of song to unearthly places. It
seems to have been likewise with the medieval hermit who penned
the following lines translated by Robin Flower:

> Learned music sings the lark,
> I leave my cell to listen;

His open beak spills music, hark!
Where heaven's bright cloudlets glisten.

And so I'll sing my morning psalm
That God bright heaven may give me
And keep me in eternal calm
And from all sin relieve me.[16]

The song of winter is the nature-theme of another writer. The translator is Brendan Kennelly:

Here's my story; the stag cries,
Winter snarls as summer dies.

The wind bullies the low sun
In poor light; the seas moan.

Shapeless bracken is turning red,
The wild-goose raises its desperate head.

Birds' wings freeze where fields are hoary.
The world is ice. That's my story.[17]

There is a very beautiful series of poems ascribed to *Suibhne Geilt* – the mad king *Suibhne* or Sweeney who lost his mind at the sight of so many broken bodies on the battlefield. The material is from the eighth century. The following poem, translated by Frank O'Connor, gives Suibhne's reflections as he flees the battlefield:

Endless over the water
Birds of the Bann are singing;
Sweeter to me their voices
Than any churchbell ringing.

Over the plain of Moyra
Under the heels of foemen
I saw my people broken
As flax is scutched by women.

But the cries I hear by Derry
Are not of men triumphant;
I hear their calling in the evening,
Swans calm and exultant.

I hear the stag's belling
Over the valley's steepness;
No music on the earth
Can move me like its sweetness.

Christ, Christ hear me!
Christ, Christ of thy meekness!
Christ, Christ love me!
Sever me not from thy sweetness![18]

Coming through the nature poetry and nature stories there is a wonderful delicacy and spirit of gentleness as well as a warmth and comfortableness. Not lacking either is a wry sense of humour, so well illustrated by many legends in the saints 'Lives'. One such mediaeval manuscript 'Life' is that of St Cíaran of Saighir, a fifth-century monk on the Offaly-Tipperary border. Consider this excerpt from Plummer's translation:

> God did many mighty works there (at Saighir) for Cíaran. When he began to dig the cemetery all by himself, he saw a wild boar coming towards him, which began to cut and root, and with this rooting it cut down the whole wood, and turned up the ground, and levelled it. Afterwards he made a hut in which to stay while engaged on that great work, the wild animal cutting and dragging the timber for him till it was finished. God gave additional monks to Cíaran, and he saw coming to them a wolf with a badger and a fox in his train, and they remained with him doing him duty and service.

> Thus they remained for a long time in this service, till it befell that the fox's native character came uppermost in his mind, and he stole Cíaran's shoes and fled to his earth den. As soon as Cíaran missed them, he said to the other monks, to the wolf and to the badger: 'It is no fit practice for a monk,' said he, 'to plunder and steal; and go,' said he to the badger, 'and bring him with thee willingly or by force, that he may be reprimanded for it.' Then the badger set out and overtook the fox, and he bound him from his ear to his tail, and brought him with him by force. Cíaran said to him: 'Fast, and do penance, for such ill conduct is no fit practice for a monk, and be sensible, and if you have any longings, God will give you as you shall desire.' He did as

Cíaran bade, and remained under the same service (as before), so that the name of God and of Cíaran was magnified thereby.[19]

The ninth-century Irish theologian, scholar, poet, and musician, Sedulius of Liege, wrote sublime religious verses in the Latin tongue but on occasion was not beyond indulging in some humorous playfulness. In the following lines he extols the piety and wisdom of a ram that was savaged to death by dogs:

He told no lies nor uttered platitudes vain.
Through báá and béé, he lilted a mystic strain![20]

And having delivered himself of that eulogy, Sedulius fills in the time before dinner by conducting the funeral rites of the ram cooking in the pot. Of course the poet, like many of his Celtic contemporaries at home and on the continent, was a *'character'*; and few can describe him better than he does himself in a short poem translated by Helen Waddell:

I read or write, I teach or wonder what is truth,
I call upon my God by night and day.
I eat and freely drink, I make my rhymes,
And snoring sleep, or vigil keep and pray.
And very ware of all my shame I am;
O Mary, Christ, have mercy on your man.[21]

But to return to the Celtic love of nature, Helen Waddell herself has a poignant poem on her relationship with the mountains she loved so well, *'The Mournes'*:

I shall not go to heaven when I die.
But if they let me be
I think I'll take a road I used to know
That goes by Slieve-na-garagh and the sea.
And all day breasting me the wind will blow,
And I'll hear nothing but the peewit's cry
And the sea talking in the caves below.
I think it will be winter when I die
(For no one from the North could die in spring)
And all the heather will be dead and grey,
And the bog-cotton will have blown away,
And there will be no yellow on the whin.

But I shall smell the peat,
And when it's almost dark I'll set my feet
Where a white track goes glimmering to the hills,
And see, far up, a light
– Would you think heaven could be so small a thing
As a lit window on the hills at night? –
And come in stumbling from the gloom,
Half-blind, into a firelit room.
Turn, and see you,
And there abide.

If it were true,
And if I thought that they would let me be,
I almost wish it were tonight I died.[22]

There is an extraordinary similarity between many passages in Peig Sayer's *'Reflections of an Old Woman'* and an anonymous twelfth-century poem attributed to St Columcille. Take the Columcille poem as translated by James Carney:

I long to be in the heart of an island,
on a rocky peak, to look out often upon
the smooth surface of the sea.

To see the great waves on glittering
ocean ceaselessly chanting music to
their Father.

To watch without melancholy its smooth,
bright-bordered strand, to hear the cry of
wondrous birds – what pleasing sound!

To hear the murmur of little waves
against the rocks, to listen to the
sea-sound, like keening by a graveyard.

To watch across the watery sea its
splendid bird-flocks, to behold – greater
than any wonder - its monstrous whales.

To see the changing course of ebb
and flood; and this to be my name –
I tell a secret thing – 'He who
turned his back on Ireland.'[23]

And now consider Peig Sayer's reminiscences about her return journey to the Great Blasket Island from a pilgrimage to Wether's Well outside Tralee:

> It was a lovely night, the air was clean, full of brilliant stars and the moon shining on the sea. From time to time a sea-bird would give a cry. Inside in the black caves where the moon was not shining the seals were lamenting to themselves. I would hear, too, the murmuring of the sea running in and out through the cleft of the stones and the music of the oars cleaving the sea across to Ventry.[24]

In another one of her reminiscences she recalls a regular morning scene from her childhood. Due to the fact that there was no survivor from nine previous pregnancies, there was a significant age-gap between herself and the older members of the family, so that she envisaged herself growing up

> like a little rose in the wilderness, without for company only those gems that God of Glory created, eternal praise to Him! Every early morning in the summer when the sun would show its face up over the top of Eagle Mountain I was often looking at it and at the same time making wonder of the colours in the sky around us. I remember well that there used to be little yellow, golden rays as slender roads coming to me from the top of the mountain, and that the mountain used to be red and a big belt of every colour, between white, yellow and black, around the sky and every colour giving its own appearance on the great, wet sea.[25]

Similar feeling for nature and for the unity of creation is very much part of the thought of Blathmac, the eighth-century poet of the Passion of Christ, who envisaged every living creature raising a lament for the death of their Lord:

> Tame beasts, wild beasts, birds
> had compassion on the Son of the living God;
> and every beast that the ocean covers -
> they all keened him.[26]

Some scholars tend to play down this love of nature and benign relationship with the elements, claiming that the basis for it in extant medieval literature is tenuous; that together with some delightful nature poetry there is a palpable fear of the power of the elements. But, while understanding their concern to offset the present-day shallow romanticism relating to much of what is termed Celtic, I nevertheless suggest that neither does their stance reflect the reality. It is not that the Celtic peoples lived in a world where everything in nature and the natural elements was 'a source of innocent merriment.' The relationship with nature and the elements is rather one of ongoing awe and wonder, be it at a bird building her nest or a lightning storm setting the forest ablaze. People certainly prayed earnestly for deliverance from the triple death – wounding, burning, drowning – but the fear did not turn them against nature itself. Few people knew the destructiveness of the sea better than Peig Sayers, and yet its presence all around her was a sacrament of God – the 'God of the Elements' (Rí na nDúl). When Peig spoke of 'the great wet sea,' the phrase conveyed a depth of mystery and variety: the wonder of it all, the power, the magnificence, the beauty, the terror, the sorrow, the sheer delight.

Again, while *Suibhne Geilt* was said to have been cursed and condemned to a life of hardship in the wilds, one may not legitimately conclude that the hermit's way of life in the woods or remote places was in any sense the same. Relative to the times, the hermit's cell with its simple furnishings was not the least of dwellings. While sailing the Adriatic, O'Daly, the Irish poet and Crusader, hankered after his bed of green rushes back home in Ireland. The builders of the monastery on Skellig Rock – twelve miles into the Atlantic from the Kerry coast – were so much in tune with nature that they were able to construct an enclosure wall in such a fashion as to shield the entire settlement from every puff of wind, even when the ocean rages all around.

In an earlier work on Irish spirituality, I elaborated a number of other characteristics of the tradition, notably that of hospitality both in material and spiritual matters, ascetical practices as a way of union with the sufferings of Jesus and Mary, the Celtic Irish *penchant* for pilgrimage and to be on the move, and what is probably a related matter, the lack of interest in establishing or maintaining bureaucracy. Because of a looming crisis for the Irish psyche on this latter issue, I will address it once again and add some other characteristics that may be useful for an understanding of the Celtic Irish way of life.

In chapter two of this book, we noted the Celtic lack of interest in bureaucracy and the fact that they never built a cohesive empire even when the opportunity presented itself. This is sometimes interpreted as a weakness but I tend to see it as a virtue. After all, what can be so silly as empire-building! The lack of interest in bureaucracy must always be seen over against the Celtic preference for friendly person-to-person communication. When the average Irishman wants to acquire information or get a job done, he will most likely have recourse to a person rather than a resource book. And while it is true that the Celtic church in twelfth-century Ireland fell in on itself partly through lack of organisation, it is equally true that it had come into being and flourished for centuries through the personal initiatives and energies of individuals and small groups. Such strengths and weaknesses are still with us today in both religious and civil life.

In 1973, when I was on a temporary assignment to the Irish and English-speaking Catholic civil servants in the then European Economic Community in Luxembourg, the talk of the town was a young Irish girl who was a typist in the old parliamentary building. One of her first assignments was the typing of a letter ultimately destined for the attention of an Italian commissioner on the eleventh floor of the building. In the normal course of events the young lady was expected to type the letter and leave it on a tray to be collected and multiplied by other officials, with a copy eventually finding its way to the Italian.

Knowing nothing of this ponderous bureaucracy, the typist completed her assignment, pulled it out of the typewriter and took the elevator to the eleventh floor. On entering the Italian's office she greeted him cheerily, patted him on the head and said 'Here you are, sweetheart' as she handed him the letter. In the twinkling of an eye, literally, she had cut through the entire impersonal system and focused on the person. And the commissioner, for his part, thought she was the best thing to hit the continent since St Columbanus.

An incident such as that can be taken as light entertainment, but if analysed it has important implications. It was obvious that this lady had a very different approach to life and people than that expected of her as a secretary in the European Community. And yet, when it comes to spirituality we frequently try to fit everybody and every nationality into a common trans-personal mould. For example, the fact that the same liturgical books are presented to Japanese, Latin American, Anglo-Saxon, Black African or Celt is an odd phenomenon indeed. To say the least, there is need for liberal adaptation in all instances if liturgical worship is to be truly prayer-full, and in tune with the character of a particular people.

Looking at contrasts in these islands alone, the Anglo-Saxon is known to be conservative, cool, calm, patient, imperturbable, and business-like even in the most critical circumstances. Over against the Anglo-Saxon stands the Celt, who now as in Roman times is considered eloquent, exuberant, excitable, highly artistic, and subject to extremes of emotion. A modern Irish poet, Michael Hartnett, expressed the racial difference in a homely but telling fashion in a radio interview: 'You are travelling by train in England and in the course of conversation you say you are a poet. Gradually the carriage empties. You are travelling by train in Ireland and you happen to mention that you are a poet, and your neighbour digs the hand into the inside pocket, pulls out some bits of paper and says: "I write a bit myself too."'

The Celtic or Celto-Megalithic Irish have another stark difference between themselves and their near and not so near neighbours. Beyond a shadow of a doubt the Irish are people of the night. The ignoring of this factor has for generations caused a considerable amount of disorientation to Irish monks and nuns whose respective congregations have a continental background or had fallen under continental influences. For the Irish the cant 'early to bed and early to rise makes a man healthy, wealthy and wise' is bunkum. For one thing, the Celts had no priority on being wealthy; secondly, such a programme would have negative effects on their health; and thirdly, it would not be wisdom but foolishness to go against the natural rhythm of one's entire being. To be out in the early morning may well be natural to Dutch or German or English. It is largely foreign to the Irish. But once darkness falls in Ireland, behold all is light! Since the flexibility that came in the wake of the Second Vatican

Council, therefore, the prayer-life of the average Irish member of a male or female religious community may well have improved. And it is also interesting to note the immediate and extraordinary welcome extended by the faithful to the Saturday Vigil Mass.

On the matter of hospitality, there is a curious traditional expression and it relates to the use of music. I experienced it only once in my own life but it was obviously part of the longer and broader tradition, as is evident from the rune common in both Ireland and Gaelic Scotland:

> I saw a stranger yesterday
> I put food for him in the eating place,
> Drink for him in the drinking place,
> music for him in the listening place;
>
> And in the Holy Name of the Trinity
> He blessed myself and my house,
> My possessions and my family.
>
> And the lark said as she sang:
> It is often, often, often,
> Christ comes disguised as a stranger.[27]

Although I do not remember hearing the lark singing, I have a beautiful and abiding memory of being welcomed with music as well as the offer of food and drink. It was during a mission in the parish of Ballinskelligs in west Kerry and I was doing house-to-house visitation prior to the week of preaching. The scenery was exquisite as I rose into the side of a mountain overlooking the Atlantic and Valentia Island. There was a lone house there between the mountain and the sea; and in the house there was a lone man, a retired blacksmith. He was standing at the door as I entered the yard. On seeing me, he didn't come forward in greeting, as I would have expected in that part of the country where people are so warm and hospitable. Instead, he retired into the house leaving the door still open. It was only when I got to the door that the situation unfolded for me. He had gone inside, taken down the fiddle from over the hob, and played two tunes to welcome the missioner into his house. After that he laid aside the fiddle and reached out both hands in warmest greeting.

Accompanying the hospitality of the open heart is the generous hand. Guaire, the seventh-century king of Connacht, was an admired exemplary figure because, as the storytellers so vividly put it, one of his arms was longer than the other as a result of all his giving. The Celts, as the ancient classical authors record, were not preoccupied with hoarding wealth. The Normans by contrast were acquisitive both as to material and spiritual matters. They are reputed to have followed

> The golden rule, the simple plan,
> that he can take who has the power
> And he can keep who can.

The Norman barons were well known through the late Middle Ages to have acquired not only the best land in the country for their eldest sons, but as often as not, the abbacy of the local monastery for the second son and the bishopric for the third.

The Celtic spirit was different and that difference survives to the present day. In the 1940s, two men, Tim Vaughan and Pat Murphy, lived side by side in the Cork-Kerry border village of Ballydesmond. Both were married. Both had families. Both had shops. But Tim had one advantage over his neighbour Pat. Tim not only owned a shop but had a dance-hall as well. However, on the occasions when Tim ran a dance, he always closed his own shop because he wanted his neighbour Pat to make a living too.

In January 1994, when travelling across the Irish midlands I was violently sick with migraine. At Kilbeggan, I saw a restaurant named 'The Loft'. In I went and ordered a cup of tea and a glass of water. Breda Kelly, the proprietress, observed me sitting at a table with my hand to my head. She came over and said: 'You are very stressed. Would you like to lie down for a while?' I readily accepted the offer of hospitality and followed her out of the dining room out across the yard and into her own home. She showed me a bedroom upstairs and told me to rest and that she would call me at whatever time I suggested. She was as good as her word and at the appointed time she reappeared and sent me on my way rejoicing. Breda didn't know me, nor to my knowledge had she ever seen me before, but it was obvious that I wasn't just a customer. I was a person first. As with the pagan Celts on the continent, personal needs were met before business was transacted.

When conducting a weekend programme in Cork city some years ago, Senator Micheál Cranitch of Ratduff pointed out an obvious but very illuminating linguistic detail in relation to the old Gaelic world. He had noted that there is no word in the Irish language for 'private property' and there is no verb 'to possess'. The term for one's property is *'mo chuid'* – my portion; the underlying social and legal position being that the wealth of the community was owned by the community and out of that resource each got enough to live on. It is a concept totally at variance with consumerist values and the cultivation of greed. When Pope Paul VI published his magnificent and revolutionary social document, *'Populorum Progressio'* (*On the Development of Peoples*), which declared that 'the goods of the world are for the people of the world', I wondered if he had any inkling of the social structure of ancient Ireland.

It was Micheál Cranitch who also drew my attention to the well-known stanza of Antoine Ó Reachtabhra which is so illustrative of that non-materialistic value system:

> *Mise Raifteiri, an file,*
> *Lán dóchais is grá*
> *Le súilí gan solas,*
> *Le ciúineas gan crá.*
> *Ag dul siar ar m'aistear*
> *Le solas mo chroí.*

> I am Raftery the poet,
> full of hope and love,
> my eyes without sight,
> my mind without torment,
> going west on my journey
> by the light of my heart.[28]

Here comes the poet, in rags no doubt and probably barefoot. He is blind. He is penniless. He has no dole, no insurance, no security. He doesn't know where the next meal is going to come from; and he doesn't know where he will lay his head when the night falls. And what is he doing? Composing a song of thanksgiving for the blessings of God which lift his spirit: a full measure of hope and love, a clear conscience and a light heart. It was out of this freedom from material pursuits and a profound trust in God that there emerged in Ireland 'an exultant spirituality'– the phrase is Brendan Kennelly's. One can travel light and celebrate the unfolding journey in thanksgiving.

Modern society, and modern Ireland, has a problem with praise. Writers tend to belittle rather than enhance the significance of the person or subject being treated. Reductive analysis – explaining things in a manner that explains them away – seems to be the vogue. This incapacity to praise is linked to unbelief. A. M. Alchin writes: 'To praise another human being or any part of God's creation means to recognize, to celebrate and to proclaim the goodness which is in them. All goodness comes from God, and is a sign of his presence in the world that he has made.'[30]

Interestingly, in spite of the current bleakness and nihilism of the Western world, artists still instinctively engage in their age-old vocation to celebrate and praise and wonder at creation. To take a Celtic example of a poet quite aware of this essential task, Dylan Thomas writes in the introduction to his 'Collected Poems' (1952): 'These poems were written for the love of Man and in praise of God, and I would be a damn fool if they weren't.'[31] Apart from its clear rootedness in the central Judaeo-Christian commandments, this statement is remarkable for its tone of bluff humour, typically Celtic in its undermining of a too-solemn approach to even the most sacred things. Nevertheless the essential seriousness remains.

During my early years in the upper Blackwater valley, the language of praise was still very strong. The teacher, Mrs Neylon, would come into school and greet the children with 'A grand fine morning, thanks be to God.' That would make good sense if the summer sun was shining in the window. But equally, she'd arrive in the heart of winter with the rain lashing across Sliabh Luachra and her coat all wet and her shoes all wet; and she'd take the wet cap off her head and shake it saying: 'A grand wet morning, thanks be to God.' For her, every morning was God's morning – hail, rain or snow, it was the gift of God; and for a gift there is only one response: thanksgiving.

In the Autumn of 1944 there was no teacher appointed to the junior section of the two-teacher school in Kiskeam. So that the term would not be entirely wasted, my parents fostered me out to Hanna Culloty and from her home I continued my education in Ballydesmond. The experience has given me an affinity with St Brendan and Columcille who were also fostered at an early age; and my foster-parent, like theirs, was also a saint. Despite that, there was the loneliness and the suppressed little sobs at prayer-time and in bed, for like my sainted friends Brendan and Columba, I was very young – only seven years old. Hanna was a young widow and a saint of God. Her language of praise still rings in my ears after half a century: 'Thanks be to God', 'Glory be to God', 'Glory, honour and praise be to the Almighty God'. These prayers of praise and thanksgiving were ever on her lips as each new day unfolded with its myriad wonders.

One of the stories my father used to tell with great relish related to a military engagement in the War of Independence. In the aftermath of Clonbanin ambush in North Cork, two volunteers called into a house for something to eat. The woman of the house spoke little but provided a fine meal at short notice. The man of the house was seated in the corner, and from his perch by the fireside he too only referred to such mundane matters as the late spring and the scarcity of hay. As the volunteers were about to depart the woman said in a low voice: 'I suppose ye were at the ambush today?' 'I suppose we were near it,' replied one of the volunteers. At that point, the old man in the corner drew the pipe from his mouth and exclaimed: 'Wisha, then boys, hadn't ye great weather for it, glory, honour and praise be to the Almighty God.' St Patrick might have frowned, but according to the '*Book of Armagh*' he did say that the Irish should always have two phrases on their lips: *Kyrie Eleison* (Lord have mercy) and *Deo Gratias* (thanks be to God). And even to this day the '*Deo Gratias*' is still heard among the people at large with a heartening frequency.

Having begun with the concept of *wonder*, it may be appropriate to end on the same note. Like John Moriarty on his hill farm in North Kerry, Patrick Kavanagh on his hill farm in East Monaghan found the beauty and the wonder of God in a cut-away bog. As with Peig Sayers, the humble flowers in their splendid but often unnoticed colours are profound revelations of *The One* – of which Kavanagh speaks:

Green, blue, yellow and red –
God is down in the swamps and marshes
Sensational as April and almost incredible the flowering of our
    catharsis.
A humble scene in a backward place
Where no one important ever looked
The raving flowers looked up in the face
Of the One and the Endless, the Mind that has baulked
The profoundest of mortals. A primrose, a violet,
A violent wild iris – but mostly anonymous performers
Yet an important occasion as the Muse at her toilet
Prepared to inform the local farmers
That beautiful, beautiful, beautiful God
Was breathing his love by a cut-away bog.[32]

CHAPTER 5

Word and Sacrament

It is hardly surprising that the Bible is the principal source and nourisher of Christian spirituality in Ireland, as it must be everywhere. That St Patrick himself was saturated in scripture is clear from his writings. And in the monasteries that soon blossomed throughout the country and became the focal points both of organization and formation in the Irish church, the Bible was the basic textbook of all learning and education. Again, this is hardly surprising, since the Gospel is the original inspiration and permanent sustainer of monastic life.

The paradigmatic figure at the beginning of monastic life is a man known now as St Anthony of Egypt or Anthony the Abbot (250-356 AD). And the paradigmatic moment of vocation in his life was when as a young Egyptian farmer at Sunday Mass he heard the Gospel reading about the rich young man who could not bring himself to leave his possessions to follow Jesus. Anthony was moved to do what the young man had failed to do and spent the rest of his long life – he is said to have lived to be a hundred and five! – in the desert, living in the spirit of the Jesus he found in the Gospel, a life of simplicity, renunciation, and prayer.

In the fourth-century monasticism spread westwards to the Mediterranean Island of Lerins off the south of France where John Cassian had a foundation; and to Trier on the Germano-Belgian border where St Athanasius established it while living in exile from his Patriarchate of Alexandria. But it was not until the emergence of St Martin of Tours that monastic life really caught fire in Western Europe. Martin had got a glimpse of monastic life during the days of Athanasius' exile. At the time he could do nothing about it as he was in the Roman army and not free to leave. Then at the age of twenty-two he was honourably discharged and pursued his dream at Lerins. About 360 AD, he established a monastery at Liguge near Potiers, in France. Ten years later, his fame was so great that he was virtually kidnapped and proclaimed Bishop of Tours. As bishop, he continued to live the monastic life and established a settlement at Marmoutier, about two miles out of the town. The success of his ventures may be gleaned from the fact that, when he died in 397 AD, there were in the region of 2,000 monks at his funeral.

According to an ancient tradition, Martin Bishop of Tours had a visit from a travelling Scotsman – none other than St Ninian. The latter had spent a decade in Rome and, according to the story, was ordained priest and bishop there before being sent back home to his own people. Sensing some of the difficulties he would have to face in Northern Britain, Martin gave his visitor an unusual and practical gift of twelve monks – skilled carpenters and masons already well schooled in the religious life.

Back home on the coast of Galloway, facing the Irish Sea, Ninian and his monks were in the process of building a stone church when word came through of the death of the Bishop of Tours, and in memory of his great friend and benefactor Ninian named the new foundation 'St Martin's'. The local Britons, however, observing this new building of a whitish stone referred to it as '*Hwith-aern*', (White House), i.e. modern Whithorn. Since Latin was widely used throughout Roman Britain and the continent, *Hwith-aern* was Latinized into '*Candida Casa*', and because of its subsequent far-reaching influence, it also enjoyed the title '*Magnum Monasterium*' – The Great Monastery.

We are dealing here with uncertain dates and sequences, but in general terms, Ninian was a generation or two ahead of St Patrick and is said to have died in 432 AD, a date traditionally associated with the arrival of St Patrick in Ireland. What is certain, however, is that '*Candida Casa*' had a strong formative influence on early Irish monastic life and consequently on the early Irish church. Many young Irishmen aspiring to religious life crossed the North Channel to study the Sacred Scriptures and Christian spirituality in The Great Monastery.

Throughout the sixth century, an extraordinary flowering of monastic life in Ireland took place under a host of dynamic and charismatic leaders such as Enda of Aran, Finian of Clonard, Ita of Limerick, Ciaran of Clonmacnoise, Comgall of Bangor, Mobi of Glasnevin, Finian of Moville, Brona of Clonbroney, Brendan of Clonfert, Jarlath of Tuam, Kevin of Glendalough, Tighearnach of Clones and, of course, Columcille of Derry and Iona. And these are but a handful of the founders and foundresses who changed the face of Ireland for ever.

The chief subject of study in the monastic schools of early Christian Ireland was the Bible. Other disciplines were considered worthwhile in so far as they advanced a better understanding and preaching of the Word of God. Consequently, the monastic spirituality which filtered through to the local Christian community was thoroughly biblical. Likewise, the Holy Sacrament of the Eucharist was treated with the greatest reverence and strict guidelines governed the appropriate celebration of sacred liturgy. Testimony to the paramount importance of both Word and Sacrament is evident in stunningly beautiful artwork in metal, stone and manuscript which have survived the ravages of a troubled history.

Young boys, fortunate enough to be launched on an educational career, began their studies as soon as they reached the use of reason. The *'Lives'* of the Irish saints indicate that this elementary stage was in the nature of an apprenticeship supervised by an individual priest or bishop. The most popular, though not the only text for learning to read was a Latin version of the *'Book of Psalms'* together with the songs (canticles) from elsewhere in the Bible. In the process of becoming literate, the young student would gradually commit the entire 150 psalms to memory. Evidence would also suggest that many monks recited the entire Psalter each day, and that on top of their manual and mental labours.

For the purpose of learning to write and take notes, the monks used little wax tablets about the size of an A4 page. These could be used over and over again because of the malleable nature of the material. It is probable, however, that most education was by oral transmission, not only because of difficulty in procuring books and materials, but also because this was the old Celtic druidic tradition of handing on information. And yet, despite the painstaking work and expense of copying, manuscripts must have been relatively plentiful as large numbers of them have survived to the present day.

Since the psalms were the source of such spiritual nourishment, commentaries on them were much in use. In the early church a lot of time and effort went into making the psalms meaningful as Christian prayers.

The Irish monks had access to the most notable commentators on the Scriptures but the most favoured of all were those of Theodore of Mopsuestia. He had a profound influence on the discipline applied by Irish biblical students. They approached the Scriptures from a literal and historical point of view rather than allowing more freedom to the imagination to find an allegorical understanding. In view of the creative imagination being so active in areas such as metalwork, manuscript illumination, and the composition of lyric poetry, one may legitimately wonder why this same talent wasn't evident in interpreting the Word of God. Was it perhaps a forestalling of what the Celtic imagination might devise?

The range of artwork on the tall stone crosses that have survived tells its own story of what was popular in relation to biblical themes. Adam and Eve, Cain and Abel, David playing the harp, Daniel in the Lion's Den are regular themes from the Old Testament. Key New Testament themes include the Presentation of the Child Jesus in the Temple, the Slaughter of the Innocents, the Baptism of the Lord, the Temptation in the Desert, the Arrest of Christ, the Triumphal (Risen) Lord on the Cross and the Last Judgment. It is thought that these crosses were painted in the bright colours still to be seen in the illuminated manuscripts, and if so, they must have been the most beautiful catechetical aids that the Christian community has ever devised.

The spirituality offered by monastic preachers may be gleaned from a variety of sermons which, in manuscript form, date as far back as the eleventh century but, in origin, may date from a considerably earlier period. The following excerpt, from a homily in the *Leabhar Breac*, is typical rather than exceptional in assigning a central and exalted place to the Bible in Christian life:

One of the noble gifts of the Holy Spirit is the Holy Scripture, by which all ignorance is enlightened, and all worldly sorrow comforted, by which all spiritual light is kindled, by which all weakness is made strong ... The divine scripture is the mother and benign nurse of all the faithful who meditate and contemplate it, and are nourished by it, until they become chosen children of God by its advice. For Wisdom (that is, the church) bountifully distributes to her children the variety of her sweetest drink, and the choicest of her spiritual food, by which they are perpetually intoxicated and cheered.[1]

Another text in the *Leabhar Breac* describes Sunday as the day for 'preaching the Word of God to the faithful out of the holy Scriptures.' And yet another enumerates the three great ways to refresh the spirit on Sundays and Feast days:

The first is the celebration and preaching of the Word of God; the second is the Sacrifice of the Body and Blood of Christ on behalf of the Christian people; the third is the giving of food and clothing to the poor and needy of the Great Lord of the elements.[2]

A Holy Thursday homily in the same *Leabhar Breac* reflects on the concept of the Body of Christ:

The commentators understand the holy Body of Christ in three ways: the first body, i.e. humanity, which was born of the Virgin Mary; the second body, i.e. the Holy Church, the perfect assembly of all believers whose head is the Saviour, Jesus Christ, Son of the Living God; the third body, the Holy Scriptures.[3]

In the Holy Scriptures, the preacher goes on, is narrated the pure mystery of the Body of Christ and of his Blood. Even the civil law of the land, the Brehon Law, reflected the centrality of Scripture and Sacrament by expressly recognising the church's duty to preach the Word and celebrate the Eucharist.

In the eighth-century *Martyrology of Tallaght*, it is laid down that 'the four books of the Gospel are to be read at mealtimes till the end of the year, a book every quarter.'[4] Special reverence was shown to the book and one might not touch it without washing the hands. In a special ceremony known as '*tocbail*' (raising up), the Bible was used in blessing and intercession for both living and dead. A monk in Tallaght by the name of Adamnan calmed monastic trouble in Clonmacnoise by raising the Gospel in the rite of 'tocbail'. Afterwards he said that 'the sign of the cross by the power of the Gospel travels quicker than the wink of an eye … and vanquishes every obstacle.' Mael Ruain of Tallaght said that 'There are three enemies attacking me, my eye, my tongue and my thoughts; the Psalter restrains them all.'[5]

Side by side with the Bible, the Holy Eucharist is central to the Christian tradition. In the Early Middle Ages, St Augustine posed himself the question as to whether the Word of God or the Body of Christ was the more important and concluded that one was not less important than the other. In the Late Middle Ages, Thomas à Kempis echoed the same sentiments: 'The Word of God is the light of my soul, and your Sacrament is the bread of life. These may be called the two tables set on the one side and on the other in the structure of the church.'[6] In his life of Columcille, Adamnan, the seventh-century abbot of Iona, uses a variety of terms for the celebration of the Holy Eucharist: 'the solemn office of the Mass', 'the mystic sacrifice', 'the consecration of the Body of Christ', 'the celebration of the Holy Mysteries of the Eucharist,' 'the consecration of the Holy Oblation'.[7]

Surviving manuscripts from the monastery at Tallaght make it possible to build up a picture of eucharistic life within a Celtic reformed monastery about the year 800. As in the wider Christian community, Sunday was paramount. It began with a preparatory vigil on Saturday evening. The highlights of the day itself were, the Sunday Eucharist (Mass), Holy Communion, a sermon, and the strict observance of the Sunday rest. The festive seasons of Easter, Pentecost and Christmas, together with other festive occasions, were celebrated with due solemnity.

It is interesting to note how the training of monks was directly linked to the liturgy. First-year students could receive Holy Communion at Christmas, second-years at Easter, third-years at both Christmas and Easter, while fourth-years could communicate at Christmas, Epiphany, Easter, Low Sunday, and Pentecost. There was a further graduation towards being able to communicate on a monthly, fortnightly and weekly basis. Although, as in the communities of St Columbanus on the continent, Communion under both species was the norm, first-years could not avail of this privilege, nor could anybody who had committed very serious sins. The Holy Eucharist was celebrated twice weekly (Sunday and Thursday), and if one happened to miss Holy Communion on Sunday, Mael Ruain, the founder of the monastery, insisted that they avail of the opportunity on Thursday 'because it was ... too long for them to wait without Communion until the Sunday following.'[8]

Both Columcille in the sixth century and Mael Ruain in the eighth were in the habit of having unconsecrated bread and wine available at the eucharistic services. This custom still prevails in certain Western and Orthodox traditions. This I discovered somewhat dramatically in Paris some years ago. When at Mass in the Russian Orthodox Cathedral of St Alexander Nevsky, I observed the faithful take Holy Communion and then partake of the unconsecrated bread and wine left conveniently on little tables. Not knowing the significance of this double event, I took Holy Communion only and was in the process of returning to my place when I was 'arrested' by a strong Russian who grabbed me tightly by the arm with one hand, and with the other pointed to the unconsecrated bread and wine. '*Pourquoi?*' said I, in my Corkonian French. 'It is the custom,' said he in heavily accented English. Feeling the vice-grip on my left biceps I put up no further resistance and partook. Later I discovered that the double action of taking the Body of Christ and the unconsecrated bread and wine was a symbol of unifying all of life, bringing sacred and secular into one.

The reverence and devotion with which the early Christian Irish surrounded the Holy Eucharist has stood the test of time. As recently as the early twentieth century, the Anglican scholar, Margaret Stokes, recorded how in a Mayo church the people would prostrate themselves at the consecration of the Mass; and when the priest raised up the host and the chalice, they would cry out '*Céad míle fáilte,*' 'a hundred thousand welcomes (Jesus)!' The long Irish Christian tradition sparkles with examples of this warm love and devotion, sometimes even at the cost of losing one's livelihood and shedding one's blood. It was the same Margaret Stokes who recounted the story of meeting with a Mayoman and berating him for the unkempt condition of the grave of a local saint from the early Christian period. The man dismissed her concern with the remark that all that was long ago. Stung by the reply, and with mounting anger, Margaret retorted that the same could be said of Jesus Christ. And to this the man calmly replied: 'Sure Christ is never long ago.'

There is another lovely custom of drinking a triple toast after partaking of the Body and Blood of Christ in the Holy Eucharist. The drink is water but the accompanying words are of the richest vintage. I got this one from a West Cork school-teacher:

> *Sláinte an Fhir áluinn do leath a ghéaga ar chrann na croise chun sinne a shaoradh.*
>
> (Health to the handsome man who spread his arms on the cross for our salvation).
>
> *Sláinte na mná mánla rug Mac ón Spioraid Naomh dúinn.*
>
> (Health to the courteous woman who had a Son by the Holy Spirit).
>
> *Sláinte Naomh Pádraig do bheannaigh Éire.*
>
> (Health to St Patrick who blessed Ireland).

Walking was the normal means of going to Mass, and in hard times this walk could be anything from ten to twenty miles. The two prayers given below are indicative of the quality of recollection with which people prepared for the Holy Celebration:

> *Siúlaimid mar aon leis an Maighdean Mhuire*
> *agus leis na daoine naofa eile*
> *a bhí ag tionlacan a hAon Mhic*
> *ar Chnoc Calbhairí.*
>
> (We walk together with the Virgin Mary
> and the other holy people
> who accompanied her only Son
> on the Hill of Calvary.)[9]

The next prayer I first heard from Micheál Ó Ceallacháin of the School of Music at University College, Cork:

> *Céad fáilte romhat, a Rí an Domhnaigh bheannaithe,*
> *a thagann chugainn le cabhair tar éis na seachtaine.*

O corruigh mo chos go moch chun A'frinn,
corruigh mo bhéal chun bréithre beannaithe,
corruigh mo chroí agus díbir an ghangaid as.
Féachaim suas ar Mhac na Banaltran
agus ar a haon-Mhac trócaireach,
mar is é fearr a cheannaigh sinn
agus gur leis féin beo is marbh sinn.

(A hundred welcomes to you, O King of the Blessed Sunday
who comes with help to us after the week.
Stir up my feet to early Mass.
Stir up my lips to blessed speech.
Stir up my heart and banish spite from it.
I look up to the Son of the Nurse,
to her only Son of Mercy
for he has so wonderfully redeemed us
and alive or dead we belong to him).[10]

At the fountain-head of that tradition of versified prayer is the old-
est surviving eucharistic hymn in Christendom, *'Sancti Venite'*. The
hymn is found in the seventh-century *Bangor Antiphonary* but is
thought to be of a much older date and specifically composed to be
sung by the faithful during the distribution of Holy Communion. It
is an exquisitely beautiful composition both in form and content.
The Antiphonary is thought to have been brought from Ireland to
Bobbio by the monk Dungal in the ninth century. There it remained
in the monastery of St Columbanus until 1606 AD when it was
transferred to the Ambrosian library in Milan where it remains to
the present day. The composition of the *'Sancti Venite'* has always
been attributed to St Secundinus (*Seachnal* or *Seachlan* in Irish), a
fifth-century companion of St Patrick on the Irish mission. It is so
beautiful that the *'Leabhar Breac'* gives it a heavenly origin, declar-
ing that while Patrick and Secundinus were going round the cemetery at Dunshaughlin, Co Meath, 'they heard a choir of angels
singing around the oblation in the church; and what they sang was
the hymn beginning *'Sancti Venite, Corpus Christi sumite'*. Hence this
hymn is sung in Ireland, when one goes to the Body of Christ, from
that time forward.'[11] Indeed, it is still sung in Ireland, but not with
the frequency that one might wish, for its rich and reverential sentiments are difficult to surpass in hymnody. The literal translation
given here with the Latin text is that of Dr Moran:[12]

San-cti ve-ni - te,   Chri-sti cor-pus su-mi-te;

San-ctum bi - ben-tes,   Quo re-dem-pti san-gui-nem

Sal-va - ti Chri-sti   Cor-po - re et san-gui-ne,

A quo re - fe - cti,   Lau-des di - ca-mus De - o.   A - men

Sancti venite,	Approach, you who are holy,
Christi corpus sumite;	Receive the body of Christ,
Sanctum bibentes,	Drinking the sacred blood
Quo redempti sanguinem.	By which you were redeemed.
Salvati Christi	Saved by the body
Corpore et sanguine,	And blood of Christ,
A quo refecti,	Now nourished by it
Laudes dicamus Deo.	Let us sing praises unto God.
Hoc sacramento,	By this sacrament
Corporis et sanguinis,	Of the body and blood,
Omnes exuti	All are rescued
Ab inferni fauchibus.	From the power of hell.
Dator salutis,	The giver of salvation,
Christus filius Dei,	Christ, the Son of God,
Mundum salvavit,	Redeemed the world
Per crucem et sanguinem.	By his cross and blood.

Pro universis	For the whole world
Immolatus Dominus,	The Lord is offered up;
Ipse sacerdos	He is at the same time
Existit et hostia.	High-priest and victim.
Lege praeceptum	In the law it is commanded
Immolari hostias:	To immolate victims:
Qua adumbratur	By it were foreshadowed
Divina mysteria.	These sacred mysteries.
Lucis indultor	The giver of all light,
Et salvator omnium,	And the Saviour of all,
Praeclaram sanctis	Now bestows upon the holy
Largitus est gratiam,	An exceeding great grace.
Accedant omnes,	Let all aproach,
Pura mente creduli;	In the pure simplicity of faith;
Sumant aeternam	Let them receive the eternal
Salutis custodiam:	Preserver of their souls:
Sanctorum custos,	The guardian of the saints,
Rector quoque Dominus,	The supreme ruler and Lord,
Vitae perennis	The bestower of eternal life,
Largitor credentibus	On those who believe in him.
Coelestem panem	To the hungry he gives to eat
Dat esurientibus;	Of the heavenly food;
De fonte vivo	To the thirsty he gives to drink
Praebet sitientibus.	From the living fountain.
Alpha et omega	The alpha and the omega,
Ipse Christus Dominus	Our Lord Christ himself
Venit venturus	Now comes he who shall
	one day come
Judicare homines.	To judge all mankind.

CHAPTER 6

A Radiant Creation

February 1st, the feast of St Brigid, is a big occasion for all who live in the vicinity of her famous shrine at Faughart, near Dundalk. On that night, a fire is lit in the old graveyard on Faughart Hill and there is a torch-light procession from there to Brigid's Shrine sheltering in the lower ground. When I made the pilgrimage myself, there was, as always, an impressive gathering of the people of God. The event commenced at eight o'clock, but for a considerable time beforehand, pilgrims were arriving on foot from all quarters. They were mostly in little groups of friends, neighbours, and, above all, families – the mother and father, sturdy teenagers, smaller children too, some of them clinging closely to the parents, others moving ahead or falling behind depending on where the interest or excitement lay. It was a pleasant night on Faughart Hill. There was no moon but a million stars lit up the sky and to some degree banished darkness from the face of the earth. In the countryside around glowed the lights of every town and village from the Gap of the North to the plains of Meath.

Be it fine day or starry night, the lovely scene on all sides of Faughart Hill must have delighted generation after generation of Christian people assembling from time immemorial to honour the saint. Even before the time of Brigid, our people may well have assembled for worship on that same spot because it is now evident that another Brigid – a goddess of that name – was widely venerated before the Nun of Kildare won the hearts of the Irish nation. *Imbolg* was the name of the pagan feast celebrated on February 1st. The word means 'giving birth,' for the feast was associated with the new life of spring – the birth of calves and lambs and the young of every bird and beast, the lengthening of the days, the sap rising in the trees and hope welling up in the human heart after the darkness of winter.

My mind was racing on Faughart Hill, for, blest though we have
been with the light of the Gospel, there is no forgetting the mystical
and reverent awareness of our pagan ancestors. It was surely their
sound human values that created the fertile soil for a spectacular
blossoming of Christianity. And traumatic as the religious change-
over must have been, they retained what was valid and truthful in
the old ways, notably a harmony with nature and a keen sense of
the rhythms of life, of 'the music of what happens.'

Since the Celts were a rural people, their faith was naturally shaped
by rural culture. But Ireland today, like the Western world in general,
is for the most part an urban society. The urban nature of society is
not in itself a problem, but the anti-human values of industrialism
and consumerism which are now so much part of urban life tend to
make a desert of the heart. As we struggle today to humanize and
Christianize our industrial and consumerist urban society, we
might learn from our pagan and Christian ancestors something of
their healing and harmonious relationship with the permanent
underlying realities of earth and sea and sky, and the changing seasons of the year.

At the beginning of each season they celebrated a major festival
which had the effect of immersing them in the spirit and reality of
the season in prospect. *Imbolg* was a Rite of Spring with all its exhil-
aration of new life. *Bealtaine,* on the 1st of May, was a rejoicing in the
warmth and pleasure of long summer days. *Lúnasa,* on the 1st of
August, introduced the hope and fertility of harvest time. *Samhain,*
on the 1st of November, attuned them to the reality of death and
decay and the long winter waiting. Whether you worship one god
or a hundred, these are permanent realities, and the annual liturgical cycle was a dynamic healing and harmonizing influence in
human life.

As I watched the priest light the fire in the old graveyard in
Faughart, I realized that St Brigid's Day, *Lá Fhéile Bríde,* is more than
a celebration of a wonderful saint of God. It is also *Imbolg,* the
rebirth of creation, the blossoming of fire out of darkness, of life out
of death. Under our feet were the dead generations. Yet in the same
earth that held them the planted seeds were already germinating,
and out of it the sap was rising in the grass and trees. A holy

woman was the focus of our devotions, but in her and beyond her we were in touch with the fertile feminine that gives birth and nourishment to us all.

After the lighting and blessing of the fire, and the blessing of the water, the procession formed. The Rosary was announced: the five glorious mysteries, a yet more wonderful celebration of life – the Resurrection, the Ascension, the Descent of the Holy Spirit, the Assumption of Mary, the Crowning of Mary as heaven's Queen. Here was real life, everlasting life, the vision that keeps us going in the hard times. In the depths of these same mysteries Brigid had lived her own life on the Plains of Kildare. And it is our belief that she still lives in those mysteries more deeply and more wonderfully than ever, now that she is totally with God in heaven.

It is possible that the concept of the four-season year may have developed from a more ancient two-season concept of summer and winter – a legacy, perhaps, of remote ancestors moving from a warmer, more southerly, climate. This possibility is reflected in the distinct emphasis given to *Bealtaine* and *Samhain* even in the four-season tradition.

At the advent of Christianity, however, a four-fold division of the year, with appropriate launching festivals, was well established. Gradually the Christian liturgical cycle subsumed and enriched the pagan cycle, without, however, obliterating it entirely. Christening, whether of a person or a culture, is a process rather than a single complete event. There are unredeemed, un-christened elements in all of us this side of paradise. The christening process may be observed rather clearly in the development of the cult of St Brigid. February 1st is no longer associated with a pagan goddess; it is the feast of a Christian saint. But the underlying devotional patterns remain essentially the same. The goddess was a guardian of domestic animals. St Brigid inherited her mantle and is still a favourite with the farming community. Her feast is the first day of spring, the farmer's New Year. Commenting on the eighth-century '*Life*' of Brigid, Dáithí Ó hÓgáin says that 'the saint is portrayed as having the power to multiply such things as butter, bacon, and milk, to bestow sheep and cattle, and to control the weather.'[1] Brigid herself is credited with the verse:

> *Gach 're lá go maith* (Every second day fine
> *Ó'm lá-sa amach*   from my day onward
> *agus leath mo lae féinigh.* and half of my own day)[2]

However, the dominant elements in popular awareness of St Brigid were undoubtedly the central Christian concerns of loving God and neighbour. While mystically united with her Lord and Saviour, she is attentive to the needs of the world around her, be it through open-handed generosity to God's poor, or a gentleness towards God's creatures great or small.

Popular prayers to St Brigid are legion. This one is a sort of incantation:

> *Cris, Cris Bríd is a Cris*
> *Muire is a Mac*
> *Bríd is a Brat*
> *Má fearr atá múid inniu*
> *Go ma seacht b'fearr*
> *a bheas muid blian ó inniu.*

> Cross, Cross, Brigid and her Cross,
> Mary and her Son,
> Brigid and her Cloak,
> Good as we are today
> May we be seven times better
> a year from now.[3]

A prayer addressed to three women saints – Brigid, Moninne and Brona – runs as follows:

> *A Bhríghid atá i bhFacairt,*
> *A Bhlinne atá i gCill-shléibhe,*
> *A Bhrónaigh atá i mBaile na Cille*
> *Go dtugaidh sibh mise go hÉirinn.*[4]

> Brigid who is in Faughart,
> Moninne who is in Killeavy,
> Brona who is in Ballinakill,
> May you bring me back to Ireland.[5]

Énrí Ó Muirgheasa, the editor of *Dánta Diaga Uladh*, has an intriguing foot-note informing the reader that the author of the above prayer was in prison in England and due to be hanged next day, though he had done nothing wrong. He said this prayer when going to bed that night and in the morning he awakened on Faughart Hill in Co Louth.[6]

Since the Celtic tradition has such a strong devotion to the person of Christ, especially in his passion and death, it is no surprise to discover that the Solemn Triduum in Holy Week held a special place. The deep theological mysteries of these days resonated beyond the church ceremonies into every crevice of ordinary life. Of Good Friday, folklorist Kevin Danagher writes:

> No blood should be shed, thus no animal or bird could be slaughtered, no wood should be worked or burned and no nail should be driven on the day on which the Saviour was crucified, while from noon until three o'clock, the period according to tradition when Christ hung on the cross, silence was observed as far as possible, and prayers were said by the whole household gathered together.[7]

Other Good Friday customs involved fasting even beyond the demands of church law; women and girls let their hair hang loose in mourning; many went barefoot; and even though no major farm work was undertaken, most people did some sowing or planting, because, as I learned in the days of my youth, 'everything sown or planted on Good Friday is guaranteed to grow'. In the Aran Islands this was the time for the *'turas'* or pilgrimage on bare feet around the whole rocky coastline of the island.

The luminous reality of the Paschal Mystery at the heart of everything is beautifully and simply captured in a well-loved poem by Joseph Mary Plunkett who was executed for his part in the struggle for Irish independence in 1916:

> I see his blood upon the rose
> And in the stars the glory of his eyes;
> His body gleams amid eternal snows,
> His tears fall from the skies.

> I see his face in every flower;
> The thunder and the singing of the birds
> Are but his voice – and carven by his power,
> Rocks are his written words.

All pathways by his feet are worn,
His strong heart stirs the ever beating sea,
His crown of thorns is twined in every thorn
His cross is every tree.

This sacramentalizing of the environment is endemic to the whole tradition and is most evident perhaps in our astonishingly large corpus of popular prayers. There are prayers to accompany almost every action and chore within and without the home and throughout one's life. Collections such as '*Ár bPaidreacha Dúchais*' (Our Native Prayers), '*Carmina Gadelica*' (Gaelic Songs/verses), and '*Amhra Coimrí*' (Protection songs) impressive as they are, can only be a fraction of the imaginative prayers, most of them in verse form, composed by the Celtic people over hundreds of years.

When the visitors had left Peig Sayers's house at night, she would smoor the fire by gathering the ashes over the live coals to preserve them till morning. In the process Peig would pray:

I preserve the fire as Christ preserves all.
Brigid at the two ends of the house,
and Mary at the centre.
The three angels and the three apostles
Who are highest in the Kingdom of Grace,
guard this house and its contents until day.[8]

I well remember my father performing the same ritual and accompanying it with prayer, but as to the words of that prayer I never asked, much to my regret now.

Among the hundreds of prayers in Diarmuid Ó Laoghaire's collection,[9] are invocations and blessings relating to coming in and going out of the house, lighting and extinguishing the lamp or candle, smooring the fire and kindling it, putting the child to bed, blessing the cow, blessing the herd, blessing the work, mending the nets, crossing a bridge or a river or the great sea.

Blowing out the candle at night brought thoughts of light eternal: 'May God never quench the light of heaven on us.' Assessing the weather prospects on an overcast day, it is said that 'if there is enough blue to make a mantle for Our Lady the day will come good.' The crowing of the cock is not 'cock-a-doodle-do', but '*Tá*

Mac-na-hÓighe-Slán' – the Son of the Virgin is risen – literally, 'the Son of the Virgin is safe.' On the way to Mass: 'Let us walk together with the Virgin Mary and the other holy people who accompanied her only Son to the Hill of Calvary.' Lighting the lamp: 'Saviour, may you give the light of heaven to every poor soul who has left this life, and every poor soul who ever prayed.' Blessing the bed: 'The cross of Christ between me and all enemies of my soul and body.' Before speaking: 'Jesus, Son of God, who was silent before Pilate, don't let us begin to wag our tongues without considering what we have to say and how to say it.' At the end of work: 'The blessing of God on the souls of the dead, and may the great God leave us our life and our health, and may God bless our work and the work of all Christians.' Baking bread: 'The bounty of God and the blessing of Patrick on all that I see and take. The bounty God gave the five loaves and two fishes, let him give to this food.' Walking: 'O God, bless every step that I am taking, and bless the ground beneath my feet.' On seeing the sunrise: 'King of the brightness and of the sun, you alone know the reason for our being, be with us every day, be with us every night, be with us every night and day, be with us every day and night.' Passing a graveyard: 'My blessing on you, Christ's faithful people, who are here awaiting the glorious resurrection. May he who suffered the Passion for your sake grant to you eternal rest.' A boatman on seeing the moon: 'Glory to you, O God of the Elements, for the bright lantern of the bay. Your own hands on the rudder and your mysterious love behind the wave.' Protection: 'The protecting circle of the God of the Elements, of gentle Christ, of the Holy Spirit, be keeping me safe.'

The author of *Dánta Diadha Uladh* gives the 'grace before meals' used by his father, and no doubt, considering the hard times he lived in, he must have often prayed it with a special earnestness:

> *Cúig aráin agus dá iasg*
> *Roinn Dia ar na cúig mhíle:*
> *Rath an Ríogh a rinne an roinn*
> *Ar ár gcuid 's ar ár gcomh-roinn.*[10]

> (Five loaves and two fish
> the Lord divided among the five thousand:
> The blessing of the King who made the division
> on our share and on our sharing)[11]

Another blessing, from Tyrone, runs:

> *Beannuigh sinne, a Dhia,*
> *Beannuigh ár mbiadh agus ár ndeoch,*
> *Ó's tú cheannuigh sinn go daor,*
> *Agus a shaothruigh sinn ó olc,*
> *Mar thug tú an chuid seo dúinn,*
> *Go dtugaidh tú dúinn cuid ar neamh.*[12]

(Bless us O Lord,
Bless our food and drink,
For you bought us dearly,
And won us over from every evil;
Since you gave us this much
May you give us a place in heaven too.)[13]

In these models there are frequent references to the Trinity, to the encircling protection of the angels and saints, and to the ultimate destiny of humankind. For example, a prayer when putting the child to bed runs: 'God bless you child. I place you under the shelter of Mary and her Son, under the shelter of Brigid and her cloak, and under the shelter of God this night.' And on putting on the light in the evening: 'O Saviour, may you give the light of heaven to every poor soul who left this world (today) and every soul for whom it is good to pray', or 'The light of heaven to our poor soul', or 'God's light and heaven to us.' On seeing the new moon: (while signing oneself with the cross) 'May God grant us the grace to enjoy it in a becoming and pleasant fashion for the benefit of our souls.'[14]

It is quickly obvious that the minds from which these prayers flowed envisoned all of life as illuminated by Gospel images just as Jesus made his Gospel incarnate in images drawn from all of life – birds flying, flowers blowing in the wind, a woman baking, a man fishing, children dancing – and in the elementary nourishers of life, bread and wine.

Is it possible for us to tune our modern urban minds to 'the music of what happens' so that we live a sacramentalized daily life? Can we similarly 'lay hold of' traffic lights, fire alarms, bus stops, microwaves, floppy discs, supermarkets and jet planes to embody the Gospel in our times? Jesus used the technology of his day in this fashion – the plough, the winnowing fan, the fishing net. To the mill of a Gospel-soaked imagination all is grist.

As for the kind of prayers or blessings appropriate for laying hold of these objects, the Celtic tradition is studded with models. For the most part, these models are simple and homely – a phrase perhaps, sometimes a rhyme, but always a raising of the mind and heart to God.

Some of the old models may need to be updated in terms of language and imagery; so like the people who have gone before us, we have to invent our own. Here are some modern models: *Lighting a fire*: 'May the light and warmth of God's love fill the hearts of all who sit by this fire.' *Before work*: 'May God bless the work of our hands and take it for his glory.' *Going on a journey*: 'Lord Jesus, be with us in our goings and comings, and keep us safe from all harm until we come home to you.' *Taking a drink*: 'May Our Lord, who changed water into wine, give joy to our hearts, and keep us thankful.' The most popular traditional prayer when taking a drink is 'May the Lord have mercy on the dead,' to which the company replies: '*Amen, a Thiarna*.' (So may it be, Lord!) And so indeed may it be, Lord! *Amen, a Thiarna!*

CHAPTER 7

Both sides of Death

It is said that the Jews know how to celebrate weddings, the Greeks birth, and the Irish death. What is said about the Irish probably applied to the Celtic world generally, but since the post-Reformation privatisation of religion, together with the rise of puritanism in the English-speaking world, the notion of celebrating death has been eroded in many places. American culture, which is heavily underpinned by puritanism, seems to have difficulty in dealing with the reality of death. Perhaps this goes back to the Founding Fathers' vision of 'the new world' and their leaving of 'the old world' of sin and death. Whatever the explanation, there does seem to be a certain avoidance of death in such phenomena as smiling corpses, musical cemeteries, and the sanitized euphemistic vocabulary of the undertakers. For persons raised in such an atmosphere it must come as a decided culture shock to go to a funeral in Belfast and perhaps be told that 'the brother of the corpse would like to have a word with you'!

What makes the celebration of death a real possibility in Ireland is the capacity to face death at two levels. There is the physical death of a person – the cold lifeless body stretched out on a bed or in a coffin – and side by side with that the faith that, though the body be a dead thing, as St Paul says, the person is living in another realm of existence. These two realities came home to me in a striking way in the not too distant past. My grandniece, Michelle, aged three, was at the funeral of my sister Eileen. The day was wet and we were filling in the grave as the assembled congregation recited the rosary. Michelle stood in silence, taking a keen interest in seeing the sodden clay shovelled in on top of the coffin. Then an adult bystander bent down to the child and pointing to the heavens whispered: 'Auntie Eileen is up there with Holy God!' 'She is not,' replied

Michelle, 'she's down there in the muck!' Both statements are true. Both fill out aspects of the human and Christian reality. It is indeed a wonderful thing to be able to live in the spirit. It is also a very healthy and necessary thing to be able to deal with the muck.

When one's understanding of reality is limited to a one-dimensional material world, being confronted with death can be scarcely anything other than an unmitigated disaster. It is different for a person who sees death as the gateway to another life and the prospect of a deeper relationship with the Lord and with so many friends 'on the other side.' When my sister Eileen was on her deathbed I witnessed a scene which reminded me of the meeting between St Patrick and the two princesses at the well of Clibhach. My sister Peggy, who was caring for her, came into the sick room one day and Eileen said: 'Before telling you anything, I want to assure you that I am of sound mind and in no way raving.' After this preface the following dialogue ensued:

> Eileen: 'I had a visitor!'
>
> Peggy: 'I didn't hear anybody coming in. Who was it?'
>
> Eileen: 'St Don Bosco.'
>
> Peggy: 'Where was he?'
>
> Eileen: 'He was standing over there by the table where John said Mass.'
>
> Peggy: 'Are you sure it was not Padre Pio?'
>
> Eileen: 'No it wasn't. Sure I know him well.'
>
> Peggy: 'How did you know it was Don Bosco?'
>
> Eileen: 'Something inside me told me.'

At no point in this conversation was there any questioning of the existence of other realms of being. That understanding solidly underpinned the entire conversation. At any rate, the visit of the saint was a wonderful consolation to the sick woman and she died the next morning.

Even to this day the community at large turns out in strength to funerals. There is a profound solidarity maintained both with the living and the dead. During a petrol shortage in the 1970s, an Irish judge, who was not well tuned in to the mood and values of the people among whom he sat in judgment, suggested that people might save fuel by refraining from attending funerals in such numbers. The poor man nearly had to leave the country!

It would not be inaccurate to say that my own father loved funerals. He grieved sorely and cried bitterly at the loss of his friends – and he had many – but with each funeral there was the gathering of the clans and all the storytelling and tracing of relationships that it entailed. He knew his own day would come too, and well I remember the night my parents sat by the fire discussing where they wished to be buried and making plans to buy the plot.

The Celtic *pietas* emerges in so many ways at a funeral, in the prayers and reminiscing at the wake, the shouldering of the coffin, the digging of the grave. Some time after one of our most illustrious pipers, Seámus Ennis, had been buried, a man walked up to his son and said: 'I dug your father's grave, and I was proud of every shovel full I took out.' Besides work on the grave, it was a privilege to be invited to shoulder the coffin. The ballad of Peter O'Neill-Crowley – a man killed during one of the many sad chapters of our history – tells how his friends secretly shouldered his coffin for about sixty miles in the dark hours of the night, and did so with love and reverence:

> Twas many a mile we shouldered you,
> *a stóirín geal mo chroí* (bright love of my heart).

In expressions such as these there is a depth of warmth and affectionate bonding that no amount of wreaths could convey. However, the complexity of modern life, coupled with the pressures of consumerism, are depriving many people of the opportunity of celebrating death in the wholesome manner to which we were accustomed. From being a very personal and neighbourly act of love and respect for both deceased and bereaved, burying the dead is becoming a consumerist business to be coldly exploited.

In my young days, most of the older women bought their habit or burial shroud and kept it in their homes in a safe dry place. At regular intervals it would be brought out for airing. In some parts of the country, the dying person would ask for the habit and place their hand on it as a sign of acceptance of death and in the belief that they gained a plenary indulgence. If they could afford it, people man-

aged to put aside 'enough money to bury them'. That was a matter of
personal dignity and honour. They not only wanted to pay their debts
during life but to ensure that there would be no unpaid debts due to
their demise. Everything was matter-of-fact. Death was something to
be faced in essentially the same practical way as other aspects of life. A
scene at Mrs Twomey's house will illustrate what I mean.

When my neighbour Mrs Twomey was dying, she asked her
daughters to light the blessed candles on either side of her bed and
this they readily did. After an interval she asked one of them to read
the *Litany of the Dying*. The daughter took up the prayer-book and
launched into the litany, but, between her unfamiliarity with the
text and the tears flowing at the death of her mother, she was making a very poor job of it. The old lady in the bed was not impressed
at the performance and finally in desperation said to the girl: 'Look
here, will you give me my glasses and I'll read it myself!'

On that occasion it was difficult to suppress some merriment. Mrs
Twomey was a widow who had seen hard times and had for long
years prepared for death by daily meditation and prayer. But there
are other situations when it is difficult to keep a straight face even in
the face of sudden or tragic death. People can be disconcertingly
concrete and direct in their speech. One night during my seminary
days in Galway we had a lecture from novelist Walter Macken. One
of his observations related to the concrete nature of popular speech,
and by way of illustration he told us the following anecdote. He
was in the Woodquay area of the city, an area which is built up for
generations past. He asked a local man if Lough Corrib once
encroached as far as Woodquay, and got the reply: 'Wasn't there a
man drowned there where you're standing.'

'Did your mother go quickly?' said I to another man. 'Like you'd
shot her!' said he. And a friend comforting a neighbour whose
mother had died suddenly said: 'You must have got a terrible
shock?' To which he replied sorrowfully: 'Not half the shock that
she got herself!'

Death can also call one's bluff. Margaret King, a Sister of Mercy,
told me of a Galway widow who was always complaining and
wishing she were dead. Her only son was weary of hearing the

same old story day after day – that she wished death would take her out of her misery. She sang this tune once too often and the son, being a resourceful young man, went out into the haggard, grabbed a rooster, plucked it clean, and then directed it into the kitchen where the woman sat. On seeing the 'naked' rooster strutting in the door she was taken aback and cried out: 'Lord Almighty, what's that?' 'It is death coming to take you, mother,' replied the young man. With that she leapt from her chair – she hadn't straightened herself for years – and pointing to her son screamed out: '*A bhás, a bhás! Ná bac liomsa ach tabhair é féin leat.*' (O Death, O Death! Don't bother about me but take him!') And there is that other little indiscretion perpetrated in Kiskeam graveyard: 'I suppose I'll be next,' said the grieving elderly widow at the grave-side of her husband. 'Well, that's what they're all saying,' retorted her undiplomatic neighbour.

Fr Jack Walsh – one of our most eminent and loveable Redemptorist missioners – used to recount how a neighbour remarked to a grieving widow: 'Isn't he a lovely corpse!' To which the widow is reputed to have replied: 'Indeed he is and the holiday in Ballybunion did him a power of good.'

In the face of death, the bereaved were always surrounded by a supportive communty which helped them express grief or any other emotion weighing heavily on them. This was facilitated by the tradition of the *caoine* – a ritualistic wailing which survived into the late twentieth century. When it began at my mother's wake in 1967, the performer was soon reduced to silence by somebody who did not appreciate its significance. Much more recently, I saw a woman arrive at the house where her mother had died suddenly. Her first expression on entering was to address the corpse with the words: 'You mean old thing, why did you do that on me!' Needless to say, with such healthy, honest and spontaneous self-expression before friends and neighbours there was no need for the organized bereavement groups such as are springing up today. The extended family and the whole neighbourhood was the bereavement group and a standard topic of conversation was the fact that the deceased 'wasn't long going in the end.' Ned Buckley – the bard of Knocknagree – composed a recitation on this very theme, and after more than half a century it is still popular in the oral tradition:

To a wakehouse I went t'other day,
God rest the poor man that was dead,
His weeping wife to me did say,
As she shook my hand 'welcome Ned.'
'His struggle is over,' said I,
'He suffered a lot, my poor friend.'
'Oh! yes,' was her tearful reply,
'But he wasn't long going in the end ...'

I moved down beside the back-door
And sat on a fine sugán chair,
The women came in by the score,
And knelt by the death-bed in prayer.
They took snuff as they rose from their knees,
From the one who was there to attend,
And they said, as they started to sneeze:
'He wasn't long going in the end ...'

When they had their drink and a smoke,
Grief seemed lifted off like a pall,
And a neighbour in the corner spoke:
'This will be the end of us all.
'Tis just thirteen months this same night,
Since he first for the doctor did send,
And started 'gainst death a hard fight
But he wasn't long going in the end ...'

In the mid-twentieth century, the custom of holding wakes, and
especially long ones, fell into some disfavour. It was said that there
were a lot of abuses at wakes in the old days. That may have been
so, but I suspect that much of the 'abuse' was nothing more than a
cultural clash between the old Gaelic ways and those of the Anglo-
Puritan culture that replaced them. By the time the wake and the
funeral had ended most people had their grieving done.

At the funeral itself, certain customs have survived for millennia,
especially customs relating to food and drink offerings buried with
the dead. For example, the placing of tobacco and a noggin of
whiskey in the coffin; or, as was observed recently in Galway, the
quiet pouring of a half bottle of whiskey on the grave by a teenage

boy who was probably unaware of the antiquity of his action or the densities of meaning in the word 'libation.' He was simply ritualizing his grief at the death of an older brother. At the cemetery of Père-Lachaise in Paris, I likewise noted many young people pouring beer on the grave of pop-singer Jim Morrison. This need for ritual continually asserts itself. In my native Kiskeam the ritual was more practical. At the funerals, two or three men established themselves unobtrusively behind a headstone close by the open grave, and instead of pouring good whiskey into the grave for the dead, poured it into glasses for the living and liberally distributed them among the faithful.

Inevitably, the world of nature has a role in death. Among the birds, the robin is particularly associated with it. In the folk tradition the presence of one or several of these little birds is thought to represent the dead. One of the touching stories from the time of the Great Famine in 1847 concerns a woman of our parish who was both kind and resourceful in finding enough food to keep people alive during that dreadful calamity. Many years later, when it came to her own funeral, a flock of robins accompanied the cortege to the graveyard and perched themselves on a bush during the burial. When the prayers were finished and the grave was filled in they flew away. And in the early medieval tradition, there is the robin that wept on the monastic Island of Darinis at the mouth of the Blackwater; when the abbot asked why he wept so, an angel informed him that St Molua was dead, and since he had never killed any creature great or small, he was mourned not only by his friends but by every living thing.

A particular quality in a rooster's crowing was interpreted in the Celtic tradition as a harbinger of death. My father would regularly announce the death of a person on the 'word' of the rooster. He was invariably right. He was also a recipient of 'the three knocks' – a not altogether enviable gift which I share with him. These knocks usually came on the window at night – but not always in the night – so that on rising in the morning he would announce that somebody bound to us by blood or friendship had died. In due course confirmation of this would come from home or abroad.

Such 'death warnings' take other forms, the best known of which is the *bean sí* or fairy woman. Though I have received the 'three knocks' more times than I can number, I have never heard the *bean sí*. However, several thoroughly reliable witnesses well known to me have described its various manifestations – a small old woman usually combing her long grey hair is perhaps the most common visible form. Another is not seen but heard – a piercing and repeated shriek which seems to come from a distance (or sometimes from under one's feet) and recedes again.[1]

The traditional burial ground of my father's people is an early Christian monastic site founded by St Finian in or about the sixth century. It is located at Nohoval between Knocknagree and Rathmore on the Cork-Kerry border and is haunted in a variety of ways, some benign, others the opposite. Late one night my father had one of these more fearful experiences, namely, that of 'the black-dog.' He was going to Rathmore to fetch the doctor for somebody who was seriously ill. Travelling by horse-and-trap, he jogged along until, at Nohoval, for the full length of the graveyard, a big black dog kept jumping up at the back of the trap, trying, it seemed, to get into it. This phenomenon ceased as soon as he had passed the graveyard.

To experience any of the above mentioned phenomena is generally accepted as a confirmation of the faith that the living and the dead are not separated from us by time or space. As far as the Celts are concerned, the otherworld and this world overlap and interpenetrate. Furthermore, the Christian understanding is that those who have gone before us are not dead at all but living in another realm of existence and not normally visible. Oftentimes, these para-normal experiences are interpreted as a request to pray for people who have departed this world since they may still have to deal with unfinished business – the broad Christian notion of purgatory. What one did on behalf of the 'Holy Souls,' as they are affectionately called, varied, as is evident from the early ninth-century *Martyrology of Tallaght*:

> Whatever one does on behalf of a dead person – be it vigil, or abstinence, or prayer of petition, or alms-giving, or frequent blessings – is of assistance to him. M'Aedóc and all his community were a full year on bread and water for the release of the soul of Brandub mac Eachach.[2]

Hence, neglecting to pray for one's dead is seen as ingratitude and a fault to be acknowledged before the Lord. The ballad of *The Croppy Boy* has a young man confess:

> I passed the churchyard one day in haste
> and forgot to pray for my mother's rest.

Consequent on all of this, the tradition is rich in prayer formulae for the dead and remembrance of the dead is a spontaneous element in many other prayers. Here is one which I got from Mr Seán Lucey, a grocer in Ballyvourney, Co Cork:

> *O a Íosa na trócaire guidhim thú*
> *As ucht do pháise agus do bháis*
> *Tabhair trócaire dom-sa atá beó*
> *Agus dos na mairbh síth agus solus.*

> (O compassionate Jesus
> For the sake of your suffering and death
> Be merciful to me who am alive
> And give peace and light to the dead)[3]

A prayer when passing a graveyard is also from Mr Lucey. It contains echoes of Alcuin's *Epitaph*:

> *Go mbeannuighidh Dia sibh agus Muire*
> *Do bhí sibh mar sinn-ne*
> *agus beimíd fós mar sibh-se.*
> *Guidhim libh-se agus go nguidhidh Dia libh agus Muire.*

> (The blessings of God and Mary on you.
> You were like us and we'll yet be like you.
> I pray that God and Mary
> May guard you)[4]

In the Celtic tradition, aside from celebrating the Holy Eucharist, the strongest prayer for the dead was considered to be the recitation of the one hundred and seventy six verses of psalm 118. The Latin text begins with the word '*Beati*' (Blessed) and for that reason the psalm is known in the Gaelic tradition as the '*Biait*.' In the fifteenth-century *Book of Lismore* there is an amusing tale concerning the intercessory benefit of praying that same *Biait* on behalf of the dead. The story goes that the abbot of Kilbeggan, in the midlands, had been discussing astrology with another monk. Afterwards, in his sleep, he saw coming towards him a nun who had died six months previously. She raised a great complaint and the abbot said to her: 'How are things there, woman?' 'Much you care,' she replied, 'discussing astrology and you not saying my requiem. Woe to you!' she said. 'What requiem do you want from me woman?' said he. 'The *Biait*, of course,' said she, 'the *Biait* after the *Biait*, the *Biait* on the *Biait*, the Biait beneath the *Biait*,' said she all in one breath, demanding that the *Biait* be recited often for her. And the text concludes: 'So there is no requiem, except the Mass for the dead, that is held in greater honour by God than the *Biait*, as was said:

> The best of wealth on earth
> and that a man give it up for his soul's sake,
> yet is God more grateful to him
> for the continual recitation of the *Biait*.[5]

The *Book of Leinster* records another reference to the *Biait*. It concerns two students sharing digs at a monastic school. On one occasion they were reflecting on death and the fact of it being a journey of no return and not even a scrap of news as to how people were faring there. With that, they made a pact that the first of them to die would come back soon afterwards with news of the other side. In due time one of them died, and after some communications difficulties succeeded in relating this message to his friend: 'Recite the *Biait* every day for my soul, for the *Biait* is the strongest ladder and chain and collar to bring a man's soul out of hell.'[6]

A legend in a mediaeval *Life* of St Senán of Scattery Island in the Shannon estuary tells how his disciple St Donnán was one day picking dilisk (sea-grass) along the shore in the company of two young aspirants to the monastic life. Their boat cut adrift and the boys were drowned but on the following day their bodies were washed ashore. The parents of the lads were very upset at the tragedy. On St Senán's instruction, the two boys were brought back to life and started to upbraid their parents for demanding their return from a land of such happiness. Their mother was astonished that they could be more happy there than at home, but the boys spoke convincingly to her: 'Mother, though you should give us power over the whole world, and all its enjoyments and delight, we should think it no different from being in prison, compared with being in this life and in the world to which we came. Do not delay us, for it is time for us to go back again to the land from which we have come; and God shall bring it about for our sake that you shall not mourn after us.' Having received the consent of the parents, the two boys accompanied Senán into the chapel where, after receiving the Sacrament of Anointing, they went to heaven. Their bodies were buried in front of the chapel and these were the first to be buried at St Senán's monastery on Scattery.[7] An interesting link across the centuries is with the glimpses of bliss reported in modern times from 'near death experiences.'

As an introduction to life in the otherworld, the anonymous eleventh-century author of *The Vision of Adhamhnán* (Adamnan Abbot of Iona) shows us the subject of his story getting a guided tour of the kingdom of heaven from his guardian angel. It is highly imaginative, with a most detailed description of the various lands of heaven, how the elect are divided into assemblies, and how they occupy themselves. The recitation of the eight canonical hours each day, together with splendid music and songs sung by saints, angels and birds, form a large part of the programme scheduled from now until doomsday. Those who did not make it to heaven are in serious trouble. They too, are divided into assemblies so that, for example, crooked lawyers, unjust judges, and heretical professors need not expect to find themselves in the same compound as unfaithful clergy, bogus healers, adulterous women and the panders who ruin them. The damned also have a full programme till doomsday, but it is one of various and continuous punishments – though with a three-hour respite on Sundays. According to Adhamhnán's vision, it is only on doomsday that the elect will finally enter the fulness of life. As for the wrongdoers, those who did not do a great deal of wrong will go to heaven on that Day of the Lord, while the rest will pass through a wall of fire to torments seven times worse than anything they have heretofore experienced.[8]

It is an immemorial custom among the Celtic bards to write their poem of repentance when they begin to feel that death is stalking them. A twelfth-century Welsh author pens his repentance thus:

O Lordly-hearted One, may there be peace between us ... and

> may I make amends for all the sins I have committed. Before
> going to my tomb, to my green grave, in the darkness without
> candle to my gravemound, to my recess, to my hiding-place, to
> my repose, after horses and trolling and pale mead, and carousal,
> and consort with women, I shall not sleep, I will take thought for
> my end.[9]

The author goes on to examine his conscience on what was expected
of him and finds himself in the company of the fool:

> The fool knows not in his heart how to tremble, he does not rise
> early, he does not pray, he does not keep vigil, he does not chant
> prayers, he does not crave mercy; pride and arrogance and
> pomp, bitterly will they be paid for in the end. He plumps his
> body but for toads and snakes and lions, and practises iniquity;
> but death will come in through the door and ravenously it will
> gather him up and carry him off. Old age and infirmity of mind
> draw nigh, your hearing, your sight, your teeth are failing, the
> skin of your fingers become wrinkled, old age and grey hairs do
> this to you. May Michael intercede for us with the Lord of heaven
> for a share of mercy.[10]

In an Irish language collection of prayers and religious lore com-
piled for me by the above mentioned Mr Lucey of Ballyvourney, I
first read the story entitled 'An Dá Anam' – The Two Souls. Eamon
Kelly, the seanachaí, has his own inimitable rendering of it in
English. According to this story, there were two 'Holy Souls' in purgatory sitting on either side of an ivy leaf, neither knowing of the
presence of the other. This particular night one of them burst out
laughing. 'Are you here long?' said the 'Soul' on the other side. 'I'm
here this past sixty years,' said he. 'And what's the cause of your
laughter?' inquired the other. 'Well,' said the laughing 'Soul', 'a
great grandson of mine has just been born; and his grandson is
going to become a priest, and he's going to offer up his first Mass
for the dead of his own people, and I'll be free then.' 'God help us,'
said the other, 'there is no one coming after me who will deliver
me.' 'Ah! don't be saying things like that,' said the happy 'Soul', 'I'll
share with you the benefit I'll get from the Mass.'

Meanwhile, up in heaven, Jesus and his mother were out walking.
'Did you hear that?' she said, referring to the conversation in purga-

tory. 'I did,' he replied. 'Well, what are you going to do about it?'
she continued. 'I suppose I'll have to do something ,' said he. So
Our Lady put sheets out airing, and that night, as Eamon Kelly tells
it, 'there were two more Corkmen in heaven!'

The upheaval in the church following on Vatican II was a source of
deep distress to my godmother, Teresa Coen. She was in her eight-
ies at the time and much of what she was hearing and reading
greatly disturbed her faith. She was just clinging on as best she
could to the tradition of faith and practice which she had known
and loved. Then one night she had a dream which cheered her up
beyond measure. In the dream she was climbing a steep and lofty
mountain. The going was tough. She was panting and wanted to
give up. But at the top of the mountain there was a group of people
urging her on: 'Come on Teresa! Don't give up! Come on, we're
waiting for you!' With this encouragement she struggled on and as
she neared the top she could see them more clearly – their joyous
faces, their hands outstretched towards her. Better still, she recognized those faces – her mother and many brothers and sisters were
there; so too was the late local doctor and many friends and neighbours whom she had known and loved. With a few more puffs and
pants and struggling steps she reached the summit. Her waiting
friends encircled her, and together with the rest Teresa jumped for
joy before being whisked into the most exciting of happy dance.
With that she awoke. It was all a dream! Or was it?

CHAPTER 8

The Way of Praise and Thanksgiving

There is a deep consciousness in the Celtic tradition of the universe and all of nature as being shot through with the glory of God. Such a vision finds continual expression in praise and thanksgiving. It is a vision inspired utterly by Scripture. The Christian tradition tells us that God has given us two books to read, the Bible and creation. To be ignorant of either is to be ignorant of their author.

The Bible itself refers us to the larger work. Tempted in the desert to change stones into bread, Jesus replies: 'Man does not live on bread alone, *but on every word that comes from the mouth of God.*' The metaphor he uses here is found first in the opening verses of Genesis. There the metaphysical mystery of creation is presented in the imagery of speech – God said: 'Light!' God said: 'Land and Sea!' God said: 'Sun, Moon, Stars!' God *speaks* creation into existence.

In the act of speech something that is within is uttered (originally *outered*), or expressed (i.e. pushed out), and becomes word. In the rich imagery of Genesis, therefore, everything that exists is a word of God, the 'outering' or expression of God's mind and heart.

The reply of Jesus to the tempter in the desert presumes this under-standing of creation. It says in effect: my Father has expressed him-self here in stones and sand. I accept these words of love and will not ask him to change them. I know I will find life in them.

Letting the mind of Christ be in us, as St Paul urges, includes learning to read the book of creation as he did, that is, walking through the world with all our senses open, taking in all the words of God, let-ting them be their unique and shining selves, letting them nourish us and delight us, letting them awaken our hearts to praise and thanksgiving. Our Celtic ancestors learned this lesson well. To them everything had a quality of sacredness and was transparent to the creator. We find it in the large quantity of nature poetry coming to us from the ninth century and earlier – the hermit alone in the woods, reading his psalms, listening to the birds, celebrating the Holy Eucharist – all is of a piece, the seamless robe of creation, rent and torn here and there by sin but essentially sound. At its best, the Celtic tradition had an instinct for this – the unity of all things – the sense of the world of nature being shot through with the grace of God. 'God saw all that he had made, and it was indeed very good' (Gen 1:31). There is, for example, that exquisite poem ascribed to Manchin Leith (d. 665 AD) but probably dating from the ninth century, where the writer envisages a little house in the woods, facing south to benefit from the sun, with bird-song everywhere but especially a lark singing overhead; clear water running by, a shining candle above the pure white Scriptures and he himself praying to God in every place. In such writings the sweetness of a grace-filled world comes through:

I wish, O Son of the Living God, ancient eternal King, for a secret hut in the wilderness that it may be my dwelling.

A very blue shallow well to be beside it, a clear pool for washing away sins through the grace of the Holy Spirit.

A beautiful wood close by around it on every side, for the nurture of many-voiced birds, to shelter and hide in it.

Facing the south for warmth, a little stream across its enclosure, a choice ground with abundant bounties which would be good for every plant.

A few sage disciples – I will tell their number – humble and obedient, to pray to the King.

Four threes, three fours, ready for every need, two sixes in the church, both south and north.

Six couples in addition to me myself, praying through the long ages to the King who moves the sun.

A lovely church decked with linen, a dwelling for God of heaven; then, bright candles over the holy white Scriptures.

One room to go to for the care of the body, without ribaldry, without boasting, without meditation of evil.

This is the housekeeping I would get. I would choose it without concealing. Fragrant fresh leeks, hens, salmon, trout, bees.

My fill of clothing and of food from the King of good fame, and for me to be sitting for a while praying to God in every place.[1]

Then you get a beautiful poem like 'Lon Doire An Chairn' – a poem from the *Fiannaíocht* tradition of the late Middle Ages. It is not overtly religious but flowing through it is the pure Christian heart rejoicing in creation. We know that its background is both Christian and monastic, and with that knowledge it reads all the lovelier because you know that it is not merely observation of a person listening to a bird:

> *Binn, sin, a luin Doire an Chairn!*
> *Ní chualas in áird san mbith*
> *Ceól ba binne ná do ghuth*
> *Agus tú fá bhun do nid.*[2]

> (O Blackbird of Cairn Wood, that's sweet!
> In all my life I never heard
> Music sweeter than your voice,
> And you at the minding of your nest.)

And so it goes on:

> O Patrick of the sweet bells!
> A pity you wouldn't listen a while
> To the sweetest music under heaven,
> And then you could return to your nones.

> It would be the same with you as with me
> If you knew the story of that bird;
> You would shed salt tears
> And you wouldn't attend to God for a while.

> In Scandinavia of the blue torrents
> MacCool of the golden goblets
> Found the bird you now see –
> There's his story for you truly.

> Cairn Wood – that wood back there
> Where the Fianna would take repose;
> Because of the beauty and grace of its trees
> They placed the blackbird there.

> The full-blooded singing of Cairn Wood's blackbird,
> The belling of the stag on Berry-Cliff,
> Music to send Fionn to early sleep,
> Ducks from The Lake of the Three Narrows.

Grouse around Conn's Royal Seat,
The otters whistling at Twin-loch Ridge,
The voice of the eagle in The Haunted Valley,
And the call of the cuckoos on Bushy Hill.

Dogs barking in the Smooth Glen,
Cry of the blind hunting eagle,
The noise of the hounds coming in early
From the Red-stone Strand.

The time Fionn and the Fianna lived
They'd prefer the mountain to the cell,
The song of the blackbird was sweet to them;
The voice of the bells not sweet.[3]

The love of nature, both leading to and flowing from the religious vision, results in 'an exultant spirituality' as poet Brendan Kennelly so beautifully expressed it.

This exultant spirituality, be it Celtic or Celto-Megalithic, has underpinned and still underpins the deepest responses in many of the people of the Celtic Fringe. The fortunes and misfortunes of centuries have taken their toll. Yet, I believe that much of it survives in the subconscious like an underground stream, and at the most unexpected times breaks the surface as a bubbling fountain. Like '*Lon Doire an Chairn*', these expressions often present themselves in secular attire, but never without that special warmth of heart and feeling, that passion and intensity that is a recognized characteristic of the Celt. To this day, in many parts of Ireland, the plight of someone in distress, even a bird or a beast, is likely to wring from the lips of a compassionate observer the expression 'Ah, the *craythur* (creature)!' God the creator is always the taken-for-granted environment, the encompassing compassion.

Surely Genesis rhymes perfectly with the extraordinary moment in the Fenian cycle when Fionn MacCumhaill asks his followers, 'What is the finest music in the world?'

'The cuckoo calling from the tree that is highest in the hedge,' cried his merry son.

'A good sound,' said Fionn. 'And Oscar,' he asked, 'what is to your mind the finest of music?'

'The top of music is the ring of a spear on a shield,' cried the stout lad.

'It is a good sound,' said Fionn.

And the other champions told their delight: the belling of a stag across water, the baying of a tuneful pack heard in the distance, the song of a lark, the laughter of a gleeful girl, or the whisper of a moved one.

'They are good sounds all,' said Fionn.

'Tell us, chief,' one ventured, 'what do you think?'

'The music of what happens,' said great Fionn, 'that is the finest music in the world.'[4]

And so indeed it is. For everything is a word – a song – of God.

Finit. Amen, a Thiarna. Finit. Alleluia.

Notes

Foreword

1. Clancy, T.O. & Márkus, G, *Iona*, (Edinburgh U.P., 1994) p 9.

CHAPTER 1

1. Sayers, Peig, *Peig – A Scéal Féin*, (Cl. an Talbóidigh Tta., Baile Átha Cliath,1936) and *Machtnamh Seana-mhná*, (Oifig an tSoláthair, Baile Átha Cliath, 1939).
2. Sayers, Peig, *An Old Woman's Reflections*, (Oxford U.P., 1972) p 115.
3. ibid., p 91.
4. ibid., p 94.
5. ibid., p 14.
6. ibid.
7. ibid., p 15.
8. ibid., p 48.
9. ibid., p 29.
10. Flower, Robin, *The Western Island*, (Oxford U.P., 1978) p 49.
11. Sayers, Peig, *An Old Woman's Reflections*, p x.
12. Flower, op. cit., p 48.
13. Ó Crohan, Tomás, *The Islandman*, (Oxford U.P., 1987) p 242.
14. ibid., p 147.
15. Flower, op. cit., p 59
16. Sayers, Peig, *An Old Woman's Reflections*, (Oxford U.P., 1972) pp 118-119.
17. Sayers, Peig, *Peig*, (Talbot Press, Dublin, 1974) p 181.
18. ibid., p 183.
19. ibid.
20. ibid., p 211.
21. Sayers, Peig, *An Old Woman's Reflections*, p xiii.
22. Sayers, Peig, *Peig*, p 176.
23. Ó Crohan, op. cit., p 240-241.

CHAPTER 2

1. Kavanagh, Patrick, *The Complete Poems*, (Goldsmith Press, Newbridge, Ireland, 1984) p 103, 'The Great Hunger'.
2. Tierney, B., 'The Celtic Ethnography of Posidonius: Translation of the Texts by Athenaeus, Diodorus, Strabo, Caesar', *Proceedings of the Royal Irish Academy* 60 (1960), pp 267.
3. Raftery, Joseph, *The Celts*, (Mercier Press, Cork, 1976) p 24.
4. Tierney, op. cit., p 247.
5. ibid.
6. ibid., p 249.
7. ibid., p 250.
8. ibid., p 249.
9. Raftery, op. cit., p 64.
10. Chadwick, Nora, *The Celts*, (Penguin Books, 1976) p 46.
11. Thomas, Charles, *Celtic Britain*, (Thames & Hudson, London, 1986) p 17.

CHAPTER 3

1. Rees, A. & B., *Celtic Heritage*, (Thames & Hudson, London, 1961) p 325.
2. Quin, B. & Cashman, S. (selectors), *The Wolfhound Book of Irish Poems*, (Wolfhound Press, Dublin, 1975).
3. O' Meara, J.J., *The Voyage of St Brendan*, (Dolmen Press, Portlaoise, 1985) pp 56-58 *passim*.
4. Stokes, Whitley, *The Tripartite Life of Patrick* (Eyre & Spottiswoode, London, 1887) p 100; Trs by J. Carney, *Mediaeval Irish Lyrics*, (Dolmen Press, Dublin, 1967) p x.
5. Stokes, op. cit., p 100.
6. Meyer, K., *Archiv für Celtische Lexikographie III*, p 232. (1906), trs Richard Tobin, CSSR.
7. Traditional: trs from the Irish by Francis Mullaghy, CSSR.
8. Mackey, J.P.(ed.), *An Introduction to Celtic Christianity*, (T&T Clark, Edinburgh, 1989) p 45.
9. ibid., p 60.
10. ibid., pp 62-63.
11. ibid., p 62.
12. ibid., pp 62-63.

13. *Ériu*, Vol. XI – Part II (1932), p 222.
14. ibid., p 223.
15. Ó Duinn, OSB, Seán, Kells Lecture, 1994.

CHAPTER 4.

1. Flower, R., *The Western Island*, (Oxford U.P., 1978) p 57.
2. Sayers, Peig, *An Old Woman's Reflections*, p 128.
3. Ó hÁinle, C., 'An Aspect of Irish Spirituality' in *The Furrow* (vol 27), 1976, p 583.
4. Mackey, J.P., *An Introduction to Celtic Christianity*, (T & T Clark) Edinburgh, 1989, p 47.
5. ibid., p 51.
6. Sayers, Peig, op. cit., p xii.
7. Allchin, A.M., *Dynamics of Tradition*, (University of Wales Press, Cardiff) p 133.
8. Keane, John B., *The Field*, (Mercier Press, Cork, 1980) pp 22-23.
9. Flower, R., *The Irish Tradition*, (Clarendon Press, Oxford, 1948) p 42.
10. ibid., p 61.
11. ibid.
12. ibid.
13. O Dwyer, Peter, O.Carm., *Célí Dé*, (Editions Táilliúra, Dublin, 1981) p 141.
14. Kavanagh, P., *The Complete Poems*, pp 22-23.
15. ibid., pp 23-24.
16. Flower, R., *The Irish Tradition*, p 54.
17. Kennelly, B., *The Penguin Book of Irish Verse*, (Penguin Books, Middlesex, 1981) p 48.
18. ibid., pp 54-55.
19. Plummer, C., *Lives of the Irish Saints*, vol. 2, (Clarendon Press, Oxford, 1922) p 100.
20. Carney, James, *Early Irish Poetry*, (Mercier Press, Cork, 1969) p 40.
21. Waddell, H., *Mediaeval Latin Lyrics*, (Penguin Books, Middlesex, 1952) p 135.
22. Corrigan, Dame Fellicitas, *Helen Waddell, a Biography*, (London, 1986) pp 222-223.
23. Carney, J., op. cit., pp 14-15.
24. Sayers, Peig, op. cit., p 79.
25. ibid., pp 129-130.

26. Irish Texts Society, Dublin, 1964, vol. 47, p 45. Trs by James Carney.

27. Trs by Seán Ó Duinn, OSB.

28. Trs by John J. Ó Ríordáin, CSSR.

29. Trs by John J. Ó Ríordáin, CSSR.

30. Allchin, A.M., *Praise Above All*, (University of Wales Press, Cardiff, 1991) p 6.

31. ibid., pp 4-5.

32. Kavanagh, P., op. cit., pp 291-292.

CHAPTER 5.

1. Maher, Ml. (ed.), *Irish Spirituality*, (Veritas, Dublin, 198), pp 33-34.

2. ibid., p 44.

3. ibid., p 34.

4. ibid., p 30.

5. ibid.

6. Kempis, Thomas à, *The Imitation of Christ*, IV,11, iv.

7. Adamnan, St, *Life of Saint Columba*, trs D. McCarthy, (Duffy, Dublin, n.d.) *passim*.

8. Maher, M., op. cit., p 31.

9. Trs John J. Ó Ríordáin, CSSR.

10. ibid.

11. Moran, Rev Dr, *The Early Irish Church*, (Duffy, Dublin, 1864) p 165.

12. ibid., pp 166-167.

CHAPTER 6

Ó hÓgáin, D., *Myth, Legend & Romance,* (Ryan Publishing, London, 1990) p 61.

2. Danagher, K., *The Year in Ireland*, (Mercier Press, Cork, 1972) p 13.

3. Oral Tradition.

4. Ó Muirgheasa, E., *Dánta Diadha Uladh*, (Oifig Díolta Foilseacháin Rialtais, Baile Átha Cliath, 1936) p 262.

5. Trs John J. Ó Ríordáin, CSSR.

6. Ó Muirgheasa, E., op. cit., p 262.

7. Danagher, K., op. cit., p 71.

8. Sayers, Peig, *An Old Woman's Reflections*, p xiv.

9. Ó Laoghaire, SJ, D., *Ár bPaidreacha Dúchais*, (F.Á.S., Baile Átha Cliath, 1975).
10. Ó Muirgheasa, E., op. cit., p 260.
11. Trs John J. Ó Ríordáin, CSSR.
12. Ó Muirgheasa, E., op. cit., p 261.
13. Trs John J. Ó Ríordáin, CSSR.
14. Ó Laoghaire, SJ, op. cit., *passim*. (Trs D. Tobin, CSSR).

CHAPTER 7

1. Lysaght, Patricia, *The Banshee*, Dublin, 1986.
2. Maher, M., op. cit., p 28.
3. Trs John J. Ó Ríordáin, CSSR.
4. ibid.
5. Ó Laoghaire, SJ, D., 'Irish Spirituality' in *The Furrow*, vol. 7(i), 1956, p 14.
6. Jackson, K.H., *A Celtic Miscellany*, (Penguin Books, Middlesex, 1980) p 287.
7. ibid., pp 285-286.
8. ibid., *vide* pp 288-295.
9. ibid., p 298.
10. ibid., pp 298-299.

CHAPTER 8

1. Green, David H., *An Anthology of Irish Literature*, vol. i, p 17.
2. Ó Canainn, P., *Filidheacht na nGaedheal*, (Press Náisiunta, B.Á.C., 1942) p 199.
3. Trs by John J. Ó Ríordáin, CSSR.
4. Montague, John (ed.), *The Faber Book of Irish Verse*, (London, 1974) pp 79-80.

Annotated Bibliography

Allchin, A.M., *Praise Above All – Discovering the Welsh Tradition*, (University of Wales Press, Cardiff, 1991). A profoundly rich and inspiring book about a little-known spirituality.

Carney, James, *Mediaeval Irish Lyrics*, (Dolmen Press, Dublin, 1967), and *Early Irish Poetry* (Mercier Press, Cork, 1965). Both books open windows on to a field of much loveliness and may draw readers into further study in this area.

Duffy, Joseph, *Patrick in his own words*, (Veritas Publications, Dublin, 1975). An attractive modern translation of the *Confessio* of St Patrick, with brief but useful commentary.

Flower, Robin., *The Irish Tradition*, (Clarendon Press, Oxford, 1948), and *The Western Island*, (Oxford U.P., 1978). These insightful books by a London journalist date from the 1940s. The former explores the Irish literary tradition from the age of St Patrick to the eighteenth century and contains the exquisite chapter entitled 'Exiles and Hermits'. The latter deals with the social side of life on the Great Blasket at the time of Peig and Ó Crohan. Both books are enhanced by the author's deep love and respect for the subject matter.

Jackson, Kenneth H., *A Celtic Miscellany*, (Penguin Books, Middlesex, 1980). A veritable pocket encyclopaedia of matters Celtic: adventure, nature, love, humour, poetry, religion – a delightful fire-side book for this world and the next!

Kavanagh, Patrick, *The Complete Poems*, (Goldsmith Press, Newbridge, Ireland, 1984). The poems from Kavanagh's pen have the earthiness and spirituality of the rural Celtic Irish.

Kennelly, Brendan, (ed.), *The Penguin Book of Irish Verse*, (Penguin Books, Middlesex, 1981). This is my favourite anthology of Irish poetry. As well as the numerous translations from the early Gaelic tradition, there is a fine selection of material down to modern times.

Mackey, James. P, (ed.), *An Introduction to Celtic Christianity*, (T & T Clark, Edinburgh, 1989). A scholarly work on Celtic Christianity in Ireland and Britain by writers from various Christian traditions.

Maher, Michael, (ed.), *Irish Spirituality*, (Veritas, Dublin, 1981). A valuable introduction to several aspects of Celtic Irish Spirituality.

Ó Crohan, Tomás, *The Islandman*, (Oxford U.P., 1987). A poignant commentary not only on Blasket Island life at the turn of the twentieth century but on life in general. Ó Crohan's famous statement – 'our likes will not be there again' – was truly prophetic.

Ó Fiaich, Tomás, *Columbanus in his own words*, (Veritas Publications, Dublin, 1974), and *Irish Cultural Influence in Europe*, (Cultural Relations Committee of Ireland, n.d.). The late Cardinal Ó Fiaich was acknowledged in Ireland and the Continent as an outstanding authority in relation to the Celtic church. This is evident from both books and makes for both interesting and satisfying reading.

Ó Laoghaire, SJ, D., *Ár bPaidreacha Dúchais*, (F.Á.S., Baile Átha Cliath, 1975). The book is a collection of close on five hundred traditional prayers from various parts of the country. *Ár bPaidreacha Dúchais* (Our Native Prayers) is only available in the Irish language.

Ó Duinn, OSB, Seán, *Amhra Coimrí – Gnásanna don Teaghleach*, (F.Á.S., Baile Átha Cliath, 1977). Another lovely collection of prayers to accompany family customs – meals, locking up, putting on the light, etc.. The book is not available in translation.

O Dwyer, Peter, *Célí Dé – Spiritual reform in Ireland 750-900* (Editions Táilliúra, Dublin, 1981). The history of the reform together with interesting detail on life in a *Célí Dé* community of the time.

Raftery, Joseph, (ed.), *The Celts*, (Mercier Press, Cork, 1976). A short and readable collection of scholarly essays on the Celts; and an excellent introduction to them.

Sayers, Peig, *Machtnamh Seana-mhná*, (Oifig an tSoláthair, Baile Átha Cliath, 1939), and *Peig – A Scéal Féin*, (Cl. an Talbóidigh Tta., Baile Átha Cliath, 1936), are the respective originals of the next two titles.

Sayers, Peig, *An Old Woman's Reflections*, trs Séamus Ennis, (Oxford U.P., 1972). A beautiful book full of spirituality and prayer.

Sayers, Peig, *Peig*, trs Bryan McMahon, (Talbot Press, Dublin, 1974). Peig's own life story embodies a whole culture and spirituality typical of much of Celtic Ireland.

Waddell, Helen, *The Wandering scholars*, (Pelican, 1954). The publication of this book in April 1927 catapulted Helen Waddell into the peak of literary society. It is a book for all seasons which opens interesting doors to people, places, ideas and ultimately to wonder and mystery.